THE BOOK OF SELF MASTERY QUOTES

Timeless Words of Wisdom About Knowing,

Changing, and Mastering Yourself

DESIGNING THE MIND

First published by Designing the Mind 2020

Copyright © 2020 by Designing the Mind, LLC.

The moral right of the author has been asserted.

ISBN 979 8 68995 933 7

PSYCHITECT'S TOOLKIT

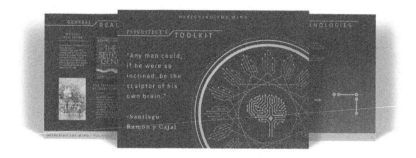

If you would like to take your pursuit of self-mastery to new heights, I write about the practice of psychitecture, or self-directed psychological evolution, which I view as the key to mastering your mind. **You can download a free, 50-page guide on psychitecture**, which includes:

•   An introduction to the basic concepts of psychitecture and psychological algorithms

•   A breakdown of 8 psychotechnologies you can start using to reprogram your mind

•   64 incredible book recommendations related to self mastery and psychitecture

•   A list of 16 websites, blogs, and podcasts that can aid in self-optimization

•   More quotes - for those who just can't get enough of them

Just go to designingthemind.org/mastery to get your Psychitect's Toolkit

INTRODUCTION

Conventional wisdom tells us that in order to be successful in life, we must build lucrative careers, impeccable social media presences, and houses full of expensive toys, smiling children, and appraisal value. Taken all together, it's a tall order, bordering on impossible. But there is a larger problem with it. The people who achieve it are often just as unhappy as when they started out. In the process of becoming what cultural prescription wanted them to be, they failed to become what they wanted to be.

But there is an alternate line of thought, one that has been echoed by virtually all of the wisest thinkers who ever lived, along with the researchers studying human well-being today. It suggests we can get off of the so-called hedonic treadmill, and onto what you might call the hedonic escalator. We can strive toward a more resilient, more powerful kind of mastery. Instead of trying to build the perfect life in which to dwell, we can fortify and master the vehicle through which we traverse it. We can live to master ourselves.

In this book, I have put together a collection of quotations and provided short commentary on each one. It is easy to write off for its simplicity, but a book of quotes, when applied, can be a powerful technology for shaping your mind. Reading the words of these legendary thinkers consistently, particularly just before starting your day, can serve as a reminder of your priorities which will color your experience throughout the day. It can weaken the hold of others people's opinions of you. It can help you to laugh at the setbacks you will inevitably encounter. And it can defend your goals and decisions from the many distractions which seek to undermine them.

There are a few important ways I wanted this compilation to stand out from other quote books. I did not want it to be a careless copy-paste of all the best known quotes on the topic. The topic of self-mastery and the thinkers who have contributed to it have personal significance for me. Self-mastery has served as a North Star for me through challenges and struggles I have faced. Many of these passages come from a collection I started years ago, and have provided me with inspiration, consolation, and meaning throughout my life. I wanted to give them away to anyone else who could find use in them.

The primary contributors to this book are not entrepreneurs and self-help gurus who have achieved mastery in business; they are the philosophers and teachers who specialized in the art of living. If you have an interest in philosophy, you will probably see some classic quotes you recognize, but I have tried to include many that will be new to readers. When possible, I provide longer excerpts to give context and to convey the meaning that was intended by the people who said or wrote them.

You might be surprised by how many celebrated quotes are misattributed or completely made up, and most quote compilations include many of these false quotes. Getting attached to a quote and then realizing it was fake can feel almost like losing a friend or getting scammed, so I have gone to significant lengths to ensure that all quotes in this book are accurately attributed. So feel free to save, share, and meditate on any of the quotes here that resonate with you with the knowledge that they are authentic. I hope you find as much value in them as I have.

REMEMBER WHAT MATTERS

"To compose our character is our duty, not to compose books, and to win, not battles and provinces, but order and tranquility in our conduct. Our great and glorious masterpiece is to live appropriately. All other things, ruling, hoarding, building, are only little appendages and props, at most."

- **Michel de Montaigne**, *The Complete Essays*

~

Are you doing enough with your life? Did you get enough done today? Have you optimized every minute of your time for maximum effectiveness? Productivity hacks are everywhere today, and along with them come the assumption that time not spent actively chasing a goal is time wasted. Michel de Montiagne understood what few others seem to - that an inability to enjoy a moment of idleness is weakness. He saw that the abilities to know, manage, and direct ourselves are our fundamental life skills. Living, being, and experiencing, are our ultimate occupations - everything else is secondary.

THE IMPORTANCE OF SELF-CONTROL

"The answer to the perennial question of what facilitates individual and cultural success might be found in the concept of self-regulation. The benefits of successful self-regulation are great and its costs can be dire. Failures of self-regulation are at the root of many personal and societal ills, such as interpersonal violence, self-defeating behaviors, substance abuse, poor health, underachievement, and obesity. The consequences of failed self-control can therefore create enormous social and economic costs, thus placing a heavy burden on society. In contrast, effective self-regulation allows individuals and cultures to thrive by promoting moral, disciplined, and virtuous behaviors."

- **Roy Baumeister**, *Willpower*

～

We are deeply conditioned to see people through the lens of pure good and evil. We feel justified in punishing criminals because we attribute their behavior to sinister motives. But Roy Baumeister, a leading psychologist studying self-control, has made the case that what we sometimes call evil is rarely a case of malicious intent. More often, harmful behaviors result from a lack of self-regulation skills, and weak "willpower muscles." If we could cultivate greater self-control in ourselves and others, many of our individual and societal issues would vanish.

THE DICHOTOMY OF CONTROL

"Of all existing things some are in our power, and others are not in our power. In our power are thought, impulse, will to get and will to avoid, and, in a word, everything which is our own doing. Things not in our power include the body, property, reputation, office, and in a word, everything which is not our own doing. Things in our power are by nature free, unhindered, untrammeled; things not in our power are weak, servile, subject to hindrance, dependent on others."

- **Epictetus**, *Enchiridion*

~~

It's a concept powerful enough to stick around for millennia, influence modern cognitive therapy, and even make it onto the wooden sign in your aunt's sunroom. Take action toward the things you have control over, and don't worry about the things you don't. Epictetus was one of the founders of Stoicism, a philosophy which urged followers not to sweat the small things, and to focus on how we respond to our circumstances over making sure they go exactly the way we want.

IT'S ALL IN YOUR HEAD

"All experiences are preceded by mind, having mind as their master, created by mind."

- **The Buddha**, *Dhammapada*

~

The Buddha was way ahead of his time. The modern mindfulness movement originates from his teachings that the thoughts, feelings, and stories which seem to color reality are nothing more than the reflexes of our minds. By cultivating an awareness of these mental phenomena, he argued, we could gradually free ourselves from their constant harassment and find peace.

THE ORGANIZING IDEA

"The organizing idea that is destined to rule keeps growing deep down - it begins to command, slowly it leads us back from side roads and wrong roads; it prepares single qualities and fitnesses that will one day prove to be indispensable as a means toward a whole - one by one, it trains all subservient capacities before giving any hint of the dominant task, goal, aim or meaning."

- **Friedrich Nietzsche**, *Ecce Homo*

~~

Do you ever feel like you're being pulled in a million directions? 19th-century philosopher Friedrich Nietzsche would say you aren't alone. He argued that a person was really just a society of desires, all competing chaotically and fighting for dominance. But for a rare person, he believed, it might be possible to find a goal so meaningful that it subordinates all desires to serve it. That person could motivate himself to achieve incredible feats and achieve a truly unified psyche.

YOUR THOUGHTS ARE TOOLS

"Man is made or unmade by himself. In the armory of thought he forges the weapons by which he destroys himself. He also fashions the tools with which he builds for himself heavenly mansions of joy and strength and peace."

- **James Allen**, *As a Man Thinketh*

~

When we think of tools, we generally think of power drills, ladders, and Mark Wahlberg. But author James Allen points out that thoughts and beliefs can serve as surprisingly powerful technologies. And learning to wield these cognitive tools will have more of an impact on your life than anything in your garage will. You can learn to avoid the self-destructive mental weapons which lead to spitefulness, shame, and self-pity, and to use empowering and positive tools to construct a palace of peace for yourself.

LOVE WHAT IS ETERNAL

"But the love towards a thing eternal and infinite alone feeds the mind with a pleasure secure from all pain... The greatest good is the knowledge of the union which the mind has with the whole of nature."

- **Baruch Spinoza**, *Ethics*

～

Losing something or someone we love can feel unbearable. But the Dutch Jewish philosopher Spinoza thought the pain of loss resulted from illusion - from a narrow window into the workings of nature. We suffer because we are unable to comprehend and love the infinite and eternal universe in its entirety. There are no divisions or distinctions in nature - no real beginnings or endings. The more you can learn to love nature as a whole, the less you will be affected by its permutations.

SEEK OUT WHAT SCARES YOU

"In short, avoiding what makes you anxious leads you to restrict your activities, which makes your anxiety generalize, which then prompts more avoidance, which in turn promotes more generalized anxiety, which stirs up even more avoidance. As you can see, it becomes a vicious cycle. The key to taming your amygdala is to break this vicious cycle. You must make sure that you expose yourself to what you were fearful of in the past. By keeping your behavioral options open to anxiety - provoking experiences, you allow yourself to be flexible and resilient in changing situations. By exposing yourself to what made you anxious in the past, you can learn to recondition yourself and habituate to the situation."

- **John B. Arden**, *Rewire Your Brain*

~~

It is a sad bit of irony that the things anxiety makes us want to avoid are exactly the things we must seek out. But this is not just an inspiring idea anymore. It's neuroscience. The amygdala, the part of our brain which acts as a smoke detector for threats, is trained through gradual exposure to fear-inducing stimuli. So whether you're afraid of public speaking, clowns, or watermelons, the key to overcoming this fear is to expose yourself to more of it. Not so much that it overwhelms you and throws you into a panic. Just enough to expand your comfort zone a little bit more.

DIRECT YOURSELF

"There are only a few who control themselves and their affairs by a guiding purpose; the rest do not proceed; they are merely swept along, like objects afloat in a river."

- **Seneca**, *Letters from a Stoic*

~

We all like to believe we have coherent reasons for our goals. But when closely examined, we often find that our aspirations are determined more by imitation than by conscious self-direction. Fortunately, goal construction is like breathing. It happens automatically by default, but can be done reflectively if we are committed to it. Seneca, another great Stoic philosopher, would urge you to wake up and ask yourself if you are truly living an authentic life or if you are merely being swept along.

REALIZE YOUR TRUE SELF

"Those whose consciousness is unified abandon all attachment to the results of action and attain supreme peace. But those whose desires are fragmented, who are selfishly attached to the results of their work, are bound in everything they do."

- Bhagavad Gita

~

Most of us can remember a time when we were fully immersed in experience without concern for how much time was passing, how much money we were making, or how we compared with other people. But it seems to get harder and harder to find this freedom as we get older. According to Hindu scripture, the path to rediscovering this freedom is found in the realization that our true identity and ultimate self is one with the eternal, all-pervasive consciousness. And by living with compassion, selflessness, and discipline, we could achieve the transcendent happiness that comes with this unification, and learn to enjoy action for its own sake, without concern for success or failure.

BEWARE THE DECOY GOALS

"The goals that you have set for yourself may be ones sold to you by the larger culture - 'Make money! Own your own home! Look great!' - and while there may be nothing wrong with striving for those things, they mask the pursuits more likely to deliver true and lasting happiness. In this case, your priority should be to discern which goals will make you happy in the long term and to follow them."

- **Sonja Lyubomirsky**, *The How of Happiness*

~

It is easy to roll our eyes when we hear phrases like "money can't buy happiness" or "looks aren't everything." But even the findings from positive psychology, the field which studies the factors of psychological well-being, consistently show that the goals prescribed by our culture are largely decoys to happiness. Psychologist Sonja Lyubomirsky argues that how happy you are has less to do with your life situation and more to do with whether you interpret it positively or negatively.

THE PLEASURE OF NECESSITY

"By pleasure we mean the absence of pain in the body and of trouble in the soul. It is not an unbroken succession of drinking bouts and of revelry, not sexual love, not the enjoyment of the fish and other delicacies of a luxurious table, which produce a pleasant life; it is sober reasoning, searching out the grounds of every choice and avoidance, and banishing those beliefs through which the greatest tumults take possession of the soul."

- **Epicurus**, *Principal Doctrines*

~

We tend to associate the word "epicurean" with extravagant cuisine and luxurious parties. But this was almost the opposite of the lifestyle proposed by the philosophical school of Epicureanism. It favored the elimination of all unnecessary desires, including those of extravagant diets and sexual pleasure. Epicurus thought the best way of being was a life of modest self-sufficiency and close friendship. Nature, he believed, made it very easy for us to be content. We only make it hard on ourselves when we overcomplicate things and long for things we don't need.

BE YOURSELF, NOT BY YOURSELF

"It is easy in the world to live after the world's opinion; it is easy in solitude to live after your own; but the great man is he who in the midst of the crowd keeps with perfect sweetness the independence of solitude."

- **Ralph Waldo Emerson**, *Self-Reliance*

~~

D o you ever feel like just running away from society and living in a ditch? Me neither, but it can be tempting to turn away from the world when contemplating the many issues and flaws it has. But Ralph Waldo Emerson, the great transcendentalist philosopher, tells us that it is more admirable to remain immersed in society, but to think and act independently, than to retreat into solitude. Be an individual. Follow your instincts. And use them to contribute to this world.

MEANING CONQUERS ALL

"The experiences of camp life show that man does have a choice of action. There were enough examples, often of a heroic nature, which proved that apathy could be overcome, irritability suppressed. Man can preserve a vestige of spiritual freedom, of independence of mind, even in such terrible conditions of psychic and physical stress."

- **Viktor Frankl**, *Man's Search for Meaning*

~~

One might assume that a prisoner in Nazi death camps during the holocaust would have only horrific stories and dark theories about human nature to share. But in addition to the terrible memories of violence and torture, 20th-century psychiatrist Victor Frankl left his camp experiences with a surprisingly optimistic theory about the human mind. He observed that whether a prisoner lost all will to live or learned to thrive in the face of his suffering was a matter of the meaning he was able to create. No matter how awful conditions seem at the time, all can be conquered by a real sense of purpose.

THE BAD CAN BE BEAUTIFUL

"Many such things will present themselves, not pleasing to every man, but only to him who has become truly familiar with nature and her works."

- **Marcus Aurelius**, *Meditations*

～

Have you ever seen a great movie and appreciated the fact that it didn't have a happy ending? Or a painting that was beautiful in the way it dealt with dark and ugly themes? We have the ability to view life as one great work of art that is made more beautiful by both the good and the bad. We can look back on our lives and feel thankful for the successes and the failures, the celebrations and the struggles. We don't have to be crushed by every change of plans if we can learn to find the beauty in what is.

DON'T BE A THOUGHT SLAVE

"I don't envision a single thing that, when unguarded, leads to such great harm as the mind. The mind, when unguarded leads to great harm."

- **The Buddha**, *Anguttara Nikaya*

~

The thought of guarding against our own minds strikes some people as odd. But the Buddha understood that the mind was the only thing that could actually hurt you. When you lack mindfulness, your thoughts will become your greatest enemy - attacking you when you're down, destroying your ability to enjoy yourself, and throwing you into ruminative spirals that are hard to escape. When you are aware of your thoughts and how they chain together and affect you, you can take that power away from them. You can become the master of your thoughts instead of their slave.

YOU ARE YOUR HABITS

"We are what we repeatedly do. Excellence, then, is not an act, but a habit."

- **Will Durant**, *The Story of Philosophy*

~~

This quote is often misattributed to Aristotle, which is understandable, because Will Durant wrote it in summary of Aristotle's ideas. Aristotle viewed a person as the sum of his habits. This understanding of habit far exceeded the narrow notion of morning routines and ingrained compulsions. An individual's entire being could be represented by his habits. His words and actions flowed from his habits, which in turn were reinforced or broken by his actions. In this way, his disposition could be cultivated and perfected. The aggregate of all his habits was his character. If you end up beating yourself up for every mistake you make, ask yourself which habits led to the mistake, and find out how you can change them.

YOUR FEELINGS DON'T CARE
ABOUT YOU

"The problem with the emotions is not that they are untamed forces or vestiges of our animal past; it is that they were designed to propagate copies of the genes that built them, rather than to promote happiness, wisdom, or moral values."

- **Steven Pinker**, *How the Mind Works*

~~

It is often argued that our emotions exist to teach us and lead us in the right direction in life. But it can be problematic to put this faith in our feelings. Our emotions exist to achieve certain purposes, but they are often at odds with our own highest goals and values. Anger may help you to fend off predators, but it can also undermine your goals. Anxiety may help you avoid dangerous situations, but it can hold you back from the most fulfilling and growth-inducing ones as well. Always take the actions you believe are best for you, whether or not they feel good at the time.

ALIGN YOUR DECISIONS AND ACTIONS

"Bad people... are in conflict with themselves; they desire one thing and will another, like the incontinent who choose harmful pleasures instead of what they themselves believe to be good."

- **Aristotle**, *Nicomachean Ethics*

~

We are all too familiar with the experience of procrastinating, cheating on our diets, and clicking "Next Episode." Aristotle believed that our character was made up of habits that could be cultivated over time. People who can't act according to their own will have been mastered by their habits. If you eat ice cream after every meal, it will form a habit which will be too strong for you to break all at once. But if you can put systems in place to decrease the bad habit one percent at a time, or replace it with a healthier habit, you can slowly near your ideal lifestyle.

YOU DON'T WANT WHAT YOU WANT

"Humans tend to anticipate more in the way of enduring satisfaction from the attainment of goals than will in fact transpire. This illusion, and the resulting mind-set of perpetual aspiration, makes sense as a product of natural selection, but it's not exactly a recipe for lifelong happiness."

- **Robert Wright**, *Why Buddhism is True*

~~

We all tend to assume we know what we want. It isn't always easy to get what we want, but surely when we do we will finally be happy. Buddhism and modern psychology agree that the things that seem like they will make us happy can be deceiving. Getting what we want often satisfies us only briefly. But somehow, it is incredibly difficult to remember how unreliable our intuitions are when it's time to make a decision. We chase after the short-term reward, get disappointed, and then do it all over again. Don't forget next time.

BEST ACTION IS NONACTION

"Great good is said to be like water,

Sustaining life with no conscious striving,

Flowing naturally, providing nourishment,

Found even in places

Which desiring man rejects."

- **Lao Tzu**, *Tao Te Ching*

~~~

Some people struggle and strain to achieve their goals. They are constantly busy. They push as hard as they can, and sometimes they succeed. But some people are able to calmly pursue goals, improve continually, and maintain balance in their lives and their minds. The legendary spiritual teacher Lao Tzu compares this way of living to water. The preeminent principle of the Tao is Wu Wei, or "nonaction," but this kind of nonaction does not indicate laziness or idleness. Wu Wei is action which is natural and intuitive, rather than forced or strained. Desire interferes with the already perfect flow of life and imposes problems which don't need to exist. Do not struggle to carry out your will, but allow action to flow through you without artificially imposing any result.

KNOW YOUR BIASES

"Before you can question your intuitions, you have to realize that what your mind's eye is looking at is an intuition—some cognitive algorithm, as seen from the inside—rather than a direct perception of the Way Things Really Are."

- **Eliezer Yudkowsky**, *Rationality*

~

We all feel certain of ourselves at times. We are wired to be confident in our beliefs, even when we don't have solid evidence for them. But the truth is even the most rational and incisive people are full of biases. These cognitive distortions systematically cause us to misperceive reality, continue to make the same mistakes repeatedly, and maintain the same unfounded confidence that we are right. Eliezer Yudkowsky, creator of the blog LessWrong, urges us not to be so trusting of our own minds. You must shift your aims from trying to be right and prove it others, to trying remove bias and gradually overcome your own limited mind.

CULTIVATE EQUANIMITY

"As a spiritual virtue, upekkha means equanimity in the face of the fluctuations of worldly fortune. It is evenness of mind, unshakeable freedom of mind, a state of inner equipoise that cannot be upset by gain and loss, honor and dishonor, praise and blame, pleasure and pain. Upekkha is freedom from all points of self-reference; it is indifference only to the demands of the ego-self with its craving for pleasure and position, not to the well-being of one's fellow human beings."

- **Bhikkhu Bodhi**, *Toward a Threshold of Understanding*

~

As we aim to master our emotions, we must attempt to cultivate the ancient ideal of equanimity. Equanimity is a state of undisturbed tranquility and psychological stability, with equivalent concepts in nearly every practical philosophy and religion - apatheia in Greek Stoicism, ataraxia in Epicureanism, and upekkha in Buddhism. Someone with this state of mind was someone whose balance of mind could not be shaken, even in the face of great adversity. Before you can masterfully maneuver your mind in the right direction, you have to learn to cultivate tranquility and keep your mind still.

KNOW YOUR WHY

"Anyone who has not groomed his life in general towards some definite end cannot possibly arrange his individual actions properly. It is impossible to put the pieces together if you do not have in your head the idea of the whole... The bowman must first know what he is aiming at: then he has to prepare hand, bow, bowstring, arrow and his drill to that end. Our projects go astray because they are not addressed to a target. No wind is right for a seaman who has no predetermined harbour."

- **Michel de Montaigne**, *The Complete Essays*

~

66 Why am I doing this?" When you don't have a cogent answer to this question, you know your goals have been set without your permission. When you insist on having reasons for your actions, you can eliminate a lot of useless fluff from your life and improve your ability to actually achieve things. When you realize that you are pursuing something arbitrary, the ends that your drives or peers or parents told you were worthwhile, you have the opportunity to take corrective measures. Don't mindlessly pursue things unless you know which harbor you are aiming for.

PRACTICE YOUR IDENTITY

"The virtues therefore are engendered in us neither by nature nor yet in violation of nature; nature gives us the capacity to receive them, and this capacity is brought to maturity by habit."

- **Aristotle**, *Nicomachean Ethics*

~

Our habits start being formed before we are able to take control of them ourselves. We acquire habits from our parents, from our siblings and peers, and from the culture we are exposed to. If you study the people with the worst behaviors, you can often find the roots of these problematic habits in their parents, or even their grandparents. But we can't resign ourselves to the habits instilled in us before we had control of ourselves. We have the power to change deeply ingrained habits and determine who we want to be, practicing this identity every day.

BECOME WHAT YOU ARE

"What does your conscience say? – 'You shall become the person you are."

- **Friedrich Nietzsche**, *The Gay Science*

~~

It seems confusing to tell someone to become who or what they are. I'm already me, right? But in a way, you aren't. In the same way a seed isn't yet a fully grown tree, but contains within it all the capacity to become one, you are not fully yourself. There are barriers within you preventing you from realizing the full potential already inside you. It is your job to break these barriers down. You have to overcome your own limiting behaviors and beliefs in order to actually become the you of your highest ideals, and this can be seen as the great challenge of your life.

YOUR LIES WILL ENSLAVE YOU

"People think that a liar gains a victory over his victim. What I've learned is that a lie is an act of self-abdication, because one surrenders one's reality to the person to whom one lies, making that person one's master, condemning oneself from then on to faking the sort of reality that person's view requires to be faked...The man who lies to the world, is the world's slave from then on...There are no white lies, there is only the blackest of destruction, and a white lie is the blackest of all."

- **Ayn Rand**, *Atlas Shrugged*

~~

When a friend asks you what you think of her singing voice, telling a white lie seems innocent enough. But when you find yourself having to sit through her Mumford & Sons cover album every time you are in the car together, Ayn Rand's point becomes clear. Not only do lies rarely help the person we lie to in the long run, they put us in the position of having to keep track of our lies and act consistently with them indefinitely. Though often done out of self-interest, dishonesty is rarely in your true best interest.

USE YOUR MIND, DON'T BE USED BY IT

"The mind is a superb instrument if used rightly. Used wrongly, however, it becomes very destructive. To put it more accurately, it is not so much that you use your mind wrongly - you usually don't use it at all. It uses you. This is the disease. You believe that you are your mind. This is the delusion. The instrument has taken you over."

- **Eckhart Tolle**, *The Power of Now*

~~~

If you find yourself constantly reliving the past or worrying about the future, there is a good chance your mind is using you like a puppet. But spiritual teacher Eckhart Tolle, shows us how to reverse this relationship. You have to recognize that the past and present don't actually exist - there is only ever one moment: now. You can learn to experience only the present moment, and enjoy blissful relief from the constant nagging of the past and future. Take control of your mind by embracing this moment.

HOW ARE YOU OVERCOMING YOURSELF

"Man is something that shall be overcome. What have you done to overcome him?"

- **Friedrich Nietzsche**, *Thus Spoke Zarathustra*

~

Nietzsche believed humans could be viewed as a hybrid between animals and something much greater. But it is up to each of us to overcome those parts of ourselves which hold us back from nearing our values. Leaving our comfort zone can be incredibly difficult, but we will never become more than we are if we don't work to climb above the plateaus we find ourselves stuck on. Which parts of your mind are limiting you? What are you doing to overcome them?

DON'T MISTAKE MEANS FOR ENDS

"Most of us are trained to watch the forward gap—the gap between where you are now and where you want to be... But there's a problem here. If you're chasing the forward gap, the chase will never end. No matter how good life gets, you'll always be chasing the next idea on the horizon. And just like the actual horizon, you can't catch it. It will always remain ahead of you. Tying happiness to the attainment of some future goal is like trying to catch up to the horizon. It's always going to be one step beyond your reach."

- **Vishen Lakhiani**, *The Code Of The Extraordinary Mind*

~

We have talked a lot about goals and setting the right ones, but Vishen Lakhiani, founder of Mindvalley, emphasizes the importance of differentiating between means goals and end goals. When we tie our happiness to means goals, we make ourselves vulnerable to situations that might not go the way we hope. But when we focus on end goals like being surrounded by love, finding ways to grow, or contributing to our community and world, our well-being will be far more resilient, and we'll be more effective in our goals too.

NEVER REMAIN STATIC

"Thus, you have within you the capacity to turn off the fight-or-flight response and the false alarms. The left prefrontal cortex and the hippocampus work together to tame the amygdala and shut down the hypothalamic-pituitary-adrenal axis. Taking action and doing something constructive can shut down the feeling of being overwhelmed, which is generated by the overreactivity of the right frontal lobe."

- **John B. Arden**, *Rewire Your Brain*

~~

It is easy to get analysis paralysis when we are anxious and have to make a decision. But making a decision, even the wrong one, is often better than making no decision at all. Taking action allows us to learn quickly and alter course if we change our mind. It also quiets our amygdala and eases our anxiety. The worst thing you can do if you're anxious is remain static, stewing in the feelings of stress and fear.

NATURE LOVES COURAGE

"Nature loves courage. You make the commitment and nature will respond to that commitment by removing impossible obstacles. Dream the impossible dream and the world will not grind you under, it will lift you up. This is the trick. This is what all these teachers and philosophers who really counted, who really touched the alchemical gold, this is what they understood. This is the shamanic dance in the waterfall. This is how magic is done. By hurling yourself into the abyss and discovering it's a feather bed."

- **Terence McKenna**, Unfolding the Stone

~~

Whether you are moving to a new city, starting a new job, or quitting your old one, leaving everything behind is difficult, and it sometimes feels impossible to plunge into the unknown with confidence that it will all work out. But one of the keys to learning to take risks is actually to learn that there isn't as much risk as you think. It is likely that the worst-case scenario for any change you are contemplating isn't death or despair, it's simply having to start back at square one with more knowledge than you started with. And best-case scenario could be far better. Overwhelmingly, the decision to let go of comfort and embrace the unknown is met with generous reward.

LOVE YOUR FATE

"My formula for greatness in a human being is amor fati: that one wants nothing to be different, not forward, not backward, not in all eternity. Not merely bear what is necessary, still less conceal it—all idealism is mendacity in the face of what is necessary—but love it."

- **Friedrich Nietzsche**, *Ecce Homo*

~

Once you have cultivated wisdom and emotion regulation skills, you develop a new type of relationship to your life. You quit expecting circumstances to go your way. You quit wanting them to go your way. You dare the world to throw you curve-balls because they make things more interesting. There are infinite paths to scale the heights of self mastery; why be attached to one? Amor fati, or the love of fate, represents an attitude of embrace. Are you capable of loving everything that happens to you, even the things that seem bad at the time?

CULTIVATE BENEVOLENCE

"What constitutes the superior man? The cultivation of himself with reverential care... When one cultivates to the utmost the capabilities of his nature and exercises them on the principle of reciprocity, he is not far from the path."

- **Confucius**, *Analects*

~~

We take for granted the golden rule "Do unto others as you would have them do unto you," but Confucius was one of the original thinkers who proposed it. He believed that if we focus on cultivating this reciprocity and regard for others, we could build better individuals, families, and kingdoms. He thought we could study the great sages of the past for more guidance on living ethically, and that benevolence was the highest virtue they extolled. He claimed that benevolence has a positive impact not only on others, but on the individual who practiced it, being the prime cause of joy.

OBSESS OVER YOUR SOFTWARE

"Your entire life runs on the software in your head—why wouldn't you obsess over optimizing it? ...And yet, not only do most of us not obsess over our own software—most of us don't even understand our own software, how it works, or why it works that way."

- **Tim Urban**, Wait but Why

~

On his excellent blog, Wait But Why, Tim Urban provides an analysis of Elon Musk, the billionaire founder of Tesla and SpaceX. He suggests a key factor of the entrepreneur's success is his ongoing endeavor to optimize his own mind. Most people strive to preserve their beliefs at all cost - to protect them from the constant threats that seek to undermine them. But for a few, all beliefs are really just temporary experiments. Every day is a mental beta test - an opportunity to iterate, expand, and upgrade your cognitive software. To uncover and question assumptions, test new conceptual models, and throw the obsolete ones out.

STUDY THE IDEALS

"[The ideal individual] bears the accidents of life with dignity and grace, making the best of his circumstances, like a skillful general who marshals his limited forces with all the strategy of war... He is his own best friend, and takes delight in privacy, whereas the man of no virtue or ability is his own worst enemy, and is afraid of solitude."

- **Aristotle**, *Nicomachean Ethics*

~~

What is the ideal person like? It seems highly subjective, but we know from studying ancient thinkers from many different cultures that there are commonalities among our values. Aristotle described an individual who was generous and caring, but remains in control of himself at all times. Someone who could be a great friend to others, but who is content to be by herself as well. These ideals are obviously not pure opinion, and studying these ancient ideals can give us great insight into our own admired qualities and values.

DEATH HANGS OVER YOU

"Do not act as if you were going to live ten thousand years. Death hangs over you. While you live, while it is in your power, be good."

- **Marcus Aurelius**, *Meditations*

~~

Marcus Aurelius's book, *Meditations*, is one of the most powerful sources of philosophical wisdom available, but not because of its innovative ideas or clever arguments. What makes this book so incredible is found in the fact that it was the Roman emperor's personal journal. It was never intended to be published. It was written by the most powerful man in the world at the time for the sole purpose of helping himself to live a better life through daily reminders of Stoic wisdom and principles. We must all learn from his commitment to living a good life, reminding ourselves that it will not last forever.

WORK ON YOUSELF FIRST

"What the superior man seeks, is in himself; what the ordinary man seeks, is in others."

- **Confucius**, *Analects*

~~~

Confucius believed the family unit was the basis of a good society, and that if we could cultivate ourselves into good family members, these good qualities would ripple outward to create a harmonious society. But the ripple effect must start with the individual. You have to work on yourself before you can improve your family, community, or world.

QUESTION EVERYTHING

"Dogmatism is the greatest of mental obstacles to human happiness."

- **Bertrand Russell**, *The Conquest of Happiness*

~~

ogmatism, or the tendency to believe what you are told without question, has greater implications than accurate beliefs about the world. Philosopher Bertrand Russell reminds us that our own flourishing can be damaged by believing without evidence. If your happiness is dependent on false beliefs, it means you have become reliant on coping structures which have been built on a bad foundation, and as soon as storms come in and reality crashes against your shoddy models of it, you'll be hit with pain and confusion. Anything that contradicts your beliefs, real world experiences or the arguments of others, will present a threat to your identity and will damage your balance of mind.

THE GREAT BATTLEFIED OF YOUR MIND

"He who is slow to anger is better than the mighty, And he who rules his spirit than he who takes a city."

- **Proverbs 16:32**, *Holy Bible, New King James Version*

~~~

We are all familiar with the ideas of loving our neighbors and forgiving others as we have been forgiven. But the Bible also asks followers to pursue self mastery. If you cannot control your own anger, you cannot expect to be able to act compassionately, especially toward your enemies. If your desires rule you, you will be easily drawn into temptation. So remember that your own mind is the great battlefield on which you must fight.

LIVE TO CHALLENGE YOURSELF

"The most intelligent men, like the strongest, find their happiness where others would find only disaster: in the labyrinth... their delight is in self-mastery... They regard a difficult task as a privilege; it is to them a recreation to play with burdens that would crush all others."

- **Friedrich Nietzsche**, *Antichrist*

~

Most of us are not eager to take on unpleasant tasks. We avoid things that cause us pain or force us to confront our own weaknesses or inner demons. But there are rare individuals who seek out these unpleasant experiences because it makes them better. The next time you are faced with what seems like an unfortunate challenge, remind yourself that you are engaging in strength training for your mind. If you actively seek out these difficult experiences, they will get harder and harder to find.

SELF AND WORLD

"We but mirror the world. All the tendencies present in the outer world are to be found in the world of our body. If we could change ourselves, the tendencies in the world would also change. As a man changes his own nature, so does the attitude of the world change towards him."

- **Mahatma Gandhi**, *Essential Writings*

~

66 Be the change you wish to see in the world" is often attributed to Gandhi, but what he actually said was deeper. There is a two way relationship between self and world. Yes, if we change ourselves, we will impact those around us and contribute to a better world. But the world, the policies, and the direct environments we are in shape us as well. So as we try to shape our environments, we must also be conscious of how the environment shapes us and choose our environment accordingly.

THE INNER CORE

"This inner core, even though it is biologically based and 'instinctoid,' is weak in certain senses rather than strong. It is easily overcome, suppressed or repressed. It may even be killed off permanently... And furthermore, these are weak, subtle and delicate, very easily drowned out by learning, by cultural expectations, by fear, by disapproval, etc. They are hard to know, rather than easy. Authentic selfhood can be defined in part as being able to hear these impulse-voices within oneself."

- **Abraham Maslow**, *Toward a Psychology of Being*

~~

One of the great humanistic psychologists, Abraham Maslow, thought each person had a biologically inscribed inner core in his mind, guiding him in the same way an acorn is guided toward becoming an oak tree. This inner core was partially unique to the individual and partially shared among all humans. And the inner core was the key to achieving deep satisfaction and the state he called self-actualization. Unlike the much louder forces of desire, this inner core could easily be ignored or neglected by the individual to his own detriment. Be sure not to mistake the two: Desires are the screams you can't ignore, but values are the whispers it is often hard to notice.

TAKE RESPONSIBILITY

"But until a person can say deeply and honestly, 'I am what I am today because of the choices I made yesterday,' that person cannot say, 'I choose otherwise.'"

- **Stephen Covey**, *The 7 Habits of Highly Effective People*

~~

One of the most common barriers to personal growth is the refusal to take responsibility for oneself. It's true that there are genetic, political, environmental, and social forces playing a part in where we end up in our lives. But many great individuals have overcome bad hands by accepting their own role in determining who they are. Though you may be a victim, living with a victim mentality will only add a second limitation to the first.

CONQUERING HUMAN NATURE

"Though one may conquer a thousand times a thousand men in battle, yet he indeed is the noblest victor who conquers himself."

- **The Buddha**, *Dhammapada*

~

The Buddha taught that ordinary human life was inherently unsatisfactory, because even when we manage to attain semi-permanent achievements, we quickly adapt to our success, and the failure to live up to our new expectations results in more pain. But he posed a solution to the cycle of torment. Nirvana was a transcendent state characterized by the extinguishment of the fire of craving and desire. If you can achieve Nirvana, you will learn to see the world beyond the conditioned perceptions and dualistic divisions imposed by your ego, to the ultimate reality of empty, ego-less awareness. You will have universal love and compassion for all conscious beings. You will experience the pinnacle of human well-being, existing only in the present moment without anxiety, selfishness, or desire.

NEVER BLAME THE LETTUCE

"When you plant lettuce, if it does not grow well, you don't blame the lettuce. You look for reasons it is not doing well. It may need fertilizer, or more water, or less sun. You never blame the lettuce. Yet if we have problems with our friends or family, we blame the other person. But if we know how to take care of them, they will grow well, like the lettuce. Blaming has no positive effect at all, nor does trying to persuade using reason and argument. That is my experience. No blame, no reasoning, no argument, just understanding. If you understand, and you show that you understand, you can love, and the situation will change."

- **Thich Nhat Hanh**, *Peace is Every Step*

~

Blame is a truly useless mindset. When we place blame on ourselves, we bury ourselves in guilt that only makes it harder to change the situation. When we blame others, we shut off our ability to empathize, understand, and build new ways to move forward. When we learn to see the many factors that contribute to who a person is and the decisions they make, we can open up the possibility of changing those factors and laying the fertilizer that will lead to new growth.

THE CENTRAL PURPOSE

"They who have no central purpose in their life fall an easy prey to petty worries, fears, troubles, and self-pitying, all of which are indications of weakness, which lead, just as surely as deliberately planned sins (though by a different route), to failure, unhappiness, and loss, for weakness cannot persist in a power evolving universe."

- **James Allen**, *As a Man Thinketh*

~

Progress can be deceptive. People can make great accomplishments without any sense of purpose behind them, and this will leave them unsatisfied and vulnerable to petty issues. The goals you achieve without a guiding purpose behind them don't count as progress. When you have this purpose, you will remain strong, motivated, and unaffected by minor setbacks.

INVINCIBLE PEOPLE

"There is no more reliable proof of greatness than to be in a state where nothing can happen to make you disturbed."

- **Seneca**, *On Anger*

~~

Have you ever met a person who was invincible? Someone who seemed never to lose his balance regardless of what happened to him. Someone who laughed when others would break down - who seemed to have a way of turning every setback into a victory without ever compromising what matters to him. This type of person is most likely the product of a rigorous endeavor to program out the uncongenial aspects of herself. When you do meet people like this, be sure to take notes.

CONTROL THE INTERPRETATION

"Remember, it is not enough to be hit or insulted to be harmed, you must believe that you are being harmed. If someone succeeds in provoking you, realize that your mind is complicit in the provocation. Which is why it is essential that we not respond impulsively to impressions; take a moment before reacting, and you will find it easier to maintain control."

- **Epictetus**, *Enchiridion*

~

Our emotions don't respond directly to outside events. Nearly all harmful emotions are filtered through our rational prefrontal cortex before reaching the emotional limbic system. The cognitive interpretation the mind forms of this stimulus is called an appraisal, and our appraisal of a situation determines our emotional response. This means anytime someone harms or insults you, you have the option to interpret it however you choose, and to avoid harm if you choose. Learn to take control of this interpretation, and you'll be untouchable.

YOUR INNER SANCTUARY

"Within you there is a stillness and sanctuary to which you can retreat at any time and be yourself, just as I can. Few people have that capacity, and yet everyone could have it."

- **Hermann Hesse**, *Siddhartha*

~~

No matter what is happening in your life, you have the option to press pause, step out of the situation, and enter the palace of your own mind. If that palace is poorly maintained, it will feel more like a prison. But if you have paid attention to it and cultivated it, it will provide you with protection, warmth, and peace.

THREE PARTS OF SELF MASTERY

"1. Use reason for its highest purpose: to evaluate and judge the best possible course of action, as free as possible from passion and bias.

2. Have an unwavering will for executing whichever actions were judged to be the best.

3. Understand that beyond clear reasoning and a resolved will, everything is outside of one's power, and should be no cause for stress or regret."

- **René Descartes**, Letter to Princess Elisabeth

~

Descartes is known for his philosophical maxim, "I think, therefore I am." What he is less known for is his ideas about the good life. He offers bits of insight in his letters to Princess Elisabeth, and here he points out that cognitive, behavioral, and emotional self mastery should be the fundamental concerns of a good life. We may not be able to control what happens to us, but we can learn to control how clearly we think, how effectively we act, and how appropriately we feel.

DECIDE WHAT TO BE

"Man does not simply exist but always decides what his existence will be, what he will become in the next moment."

- **Viktor Frankl**, *Man's Search for Meaning*

~

We are faced with countless decisions from the moment we wake up each day. What to wear, where to get coffee, and whether to send the snarky email we drafted up last night. But the most crucial decision that we have to make at each moment is who we want to be. Our actions show the world, and ourselves, who we want to be, so act wisely.

THOUGHT SUBSTITUTION

"Greed and aversion surface in the form of thoughts, and thus can be eroded by a process of 'thought substitution,' by replacing them with the thoughts opposed to them."

- **Bhikkhu Bodhi**, *The Noble Eightfold Path*

~~

Have you ever sat at a red light full of anger that it is taking too long to change? Of course you have. Have you ever been frustrated that a red light changed to green too quickly - perhaps because it interrupted your attempt to eat a sandwich or shave your legs on your commute? In this conflict, there is an opportunity. Next time you are sitting at a red light impatiently, try cultivating the desire for the light to stay red as long as possible. Try to desire the opposite of whatever is nagging at you. By generating conflicting desires, you hedge your bets against unwanted outcomes and turn every outcome into a wanted one.

DON'T REMAIN IN THE VALLEYS

"I had no idea how dull the world could sometimes be. How easy it would be to remain in the valleys, to be satisfied with mediocrity. Or how difficult it would be to stay alert to life... Being a responsible adult is, among other things, often to resign oneself to a life that falls radically short of the expectations and potentialities that one had or, indeed, still has."

- **John Kaag**, *Hiking with Nietzsche*

~

In his book, Hiking with Nietzsche, John Kaag points out that Nietzsche's philosophy is sometimes critiqued as immature and best suited for adolescence. But Kaag claims that many of Nietzsche's ideas are not only appropriate for those in the midst of adulthood, but may even be "lost on the young." Though it is true that many of Nietzsche's ideas are grandiose and dramatic, they can also be powerful reminders that one has a choice to bear the discomfort needed to do great things. He argued that the great life was the life of the individual who overcomes resistance - who overcomes one's own desire for pleasure and comfort.

NEGATIVE AUTOMATIC THOUGHTS

"Every time you feel depressed about something, try to identify a corresponding negative thought you had just prior to and during the depression. Because these thoughts have actually created your bad mood, by learning to restructure them, you can change your mood. You are probably skeptical of all this because your negative thinking has become such a part of your life that it has become automatic. For this reason I call negative thoughts "automatic thoughts." They run through your mind automatically without the slightest effort on your part to put them there. They are as obvious and natural to you as the way you hold a fork."

- **David Burns**, *Feeling Good*

~~

Cognitive behavioral therapy (CBT) is the most effective therapeutic treatment ever developed. The central idea of CBT, which will likely be familiar to you by this point in the book, is that negative feelings and moods, even disorders like anxiety and depression, are caused by automatic thoughts. Dr. David Burns teaches that you can learn to find the problematic thoughts responsible for your bad moods and restructure them for good.

COUNTER WITH THE OPPOSITE

"Conquer anger with non-anger. Conquer badness with goodness. Conquer meanness with generosity. Conquer dishonesty with truth."

- **The Buddha**, *Dhammapada*

~~

The Buddha understood that fighting fire with fire is a terrible strategy. When someone is hostile toward you, the most tempting and seemingly appropriate response is to return the anger with more anger. But not only does this action not improve the situation, it isn't even satisfying. We often regret the things we said or did while simultaneously dealing with the other person's behavior. Revenge only creates a self-perpetuating cycle of negativity, so the next time you have the urge to retaliate, do the opposite instead.

SELF-GOVERNMENT

"The perfect law would bear to individuals the same relation which perfect reason bears to passions: it would be the coordination of conflicting forces to avoid the ruin and increase the power of the whole."

- **Baruch Spinoza**, *Ethics*

~

Several philosophers have explored the parallels between the human mind and human society. There are many things we can learn from good governmental systems to aid in building better minds. If you can create a system of checks and balances that keep you from procrastinating, overeating, or drunk texting your ex, you will avoid many problems. You will become greater as a whole if you place limits on the parts.

YOU BECOME YOUR VISION

"The Vision that you glorify in your mind, the Ideal that you enthrone in your heart—this you will build your life by, this you will become."

- **James Allen**, *As a Man Thinketh*

~~

In his exceptional book, As a Man Thinketh, philosopher James Allen refers to a 'vision' or 'ideal' of supreme importance. You can think of this vision as your ideal self. If you have any hopes of becoming your best self, you must at least be able to picture it. What qualities would you use to describe this person? How do they differ from your current qualities? How can you bridge the gap?

THE PRIVILEGE OF OWNING YOURSELF

"The individual has always had to struggle to keep from being overwhelmed by the tribe. If you try it, you will be lonely often, and sometimes frightened. But no price is too high to pay for the privilege of owning yourself."

- **Rudyard Kipling**, interview with Arthur Gordon

~~

Nonconformity isn't fundamentally about talking or dressing differently from others. It's about not allowing others to take control of your choices. People can be convinced by popular opinion to make ridiculous purchases, compromise their goals, and even commit felonies. When other people want you to do something, saying no will always feel bad. But as your time and resources get more limited and your choices more impactful, 'no' can be the most powerful word.

CORRECT YOUR CONCEPTIONS

"Thus psychological problems can be mastered by sharpening discriminations, correcting misconceptions, and learning more adaptive attitudes... His problems are derived from certain distortions of reality based on erroneous premises and misconceptions."

- **Aaron Beck**, *Cognitive Therapy and the Emotional Disorders*

~

Aaron Beck was a founding father of cognitive behavioral therapy, which holds that immediately after an emotional response, our rational mind has the opportunity to reflect and reinterpret the information before it feeds back into our emotions. It must be stressed that this is not the same thing as the positive thinking which is so popular in today's self-help section. Thinking positive thoughts will not force the negative ones away, nor will suppression, the brute force "willing away" of emotion, which is ineffective and often backfires.

DON'T INDULGE YOUR FEAR

"Any action is often better than no action, especially if you have been stuck in an unhappy situation for a long time. If it is a mistake, at least you learn something, in which case it's no longer a mistake. If you remain stuck, you learn nothing. Is fear preventing you from taking action? Acknowledge the fear, watch it, take your attention into it, be fully present with it. Doing so cuts the link between the fear and your thinking. Don't let the fear rise up into your mind. Use the power of the Now. Fear cannot prevail against it."

- **Eckhart Tolle**, *The Power of Now*

~~

We have already talked about the benefit of taking action when you are afraid, but Eckhart Tolle introduces another way of dealing with fear: watch it. Don't engage with your fear or indulge its unrealistic fantasies. Observe it mindfully without judgment, and it will slowly pass. By doing this, you break the vicious cycle of anxiety.

LOG YOUR THOUGHTS

"A sense of worthlessness is created by your internal self-critical dialogue. In order to overcome this bad mental habit, three steps are necessary: a. Train yourself to recognize and write down the self-critical thoughts as they go through your mind; b. Learn why these thoughts are distorted; and c. Practice talking back to them so as to develop a more realistic self-evaluation system."

- **David Burns**, *Feeling Good*

~

If you've ever said the phrase "I can't do anything right," or "I'm a total failure" you are likely in need of the process of cognitive restructuring. This process will rewire your relationship with yourself and help you develop more accurate self-evaluations. Start with a log which tracks: the automatic thoughts you experience, the distorted reasoning in those thoughts, and the rational response you'd like to replace it with.

COMPETE WITH YOURSELF

"Therefore Sages cling to the One

And take care of this world;

Do not display themselves

And therefore shine;

Do not assert themselves

And therefore stand out;

Do not praise themselves

And therefore succeed;

Are not complacent

And therefore endure;

Do not contend

And therefore no one under heaven

Can contend with them."

- **Lao Tzu**, *Tao Te Ching*

~

Some people seem to live their entire lives like one big competition, constantly trying to beat others, brag about their accomplishments, and get as much attention as possible. The irony is that the winners of this great competition are generally the ones who aren't even playing it. If you only try to compete with and impress yourself, you will likely wake up one day to find you have left everyone else in the dust.

DESIGN YOUR LIFESTYLE

"Each individual has to find and create his/her own life style and is responsible for his or her own self-fulfillment."

- **Susanne Cook-Greuter**, *Nine Levels Of Increasing Embrace In Ego Development*

~

Susanne Cook-Greuter followed the work of Jane Loevinger studying the stages people go through in understanding the world and themselves. She found that it isn't until a rare and advanced stage that people start to consciously design their lifestyle for maximum fulfillment. Until that point, people just follow the track laid out for them by others, hoping it will lead somewhere good. If you have the ability to design a life that is fulfilling to you, don't be afraid to live it without guilt.

THE COURAGE TO INTROSPECT

"If you are irritated by every rub, how will your mirror be polished?"

- **Rumi**, *Masnavi*

~~

Looking deeper into ourselves can be disturbing, and it leads some to avoid introspection altogether. The 13th-century Persian poet, Rumi offers the perfect concise analogy for introspection and personal development. We can't grow if we are unwilling to bear the discomfort of looking honestly at ourselves. We have to be willing to ask others for feedback that will give us greater clarity into our minds. It may sting in the short-term, but it will help us to become the best version of ourselves in the long-term.

DON'T BE MANIPULATION BAIT

"He who cannot obey himself will be commanded. That is the nature of living creatures."

- **Friedrich Nietzsche**, *Thus Spoke Zarathustra*

~~

Lacking self-control will not only prevent you from achieving what you care about. It will put a neon sign on your back encouraging others to use you for their goals. If you can't differentiate truth from fiction, regulate your emotions, or exercise restraint, you will be a manipulative person's favorite tool. In addition to cultivating these strengths, learn to identify persuasion tactics so you can become resistant to the manipulation of others.

THE SMQ TEST

"We may all have been born with the capacity for willpower, but some of us use it more than others. People who have better control of their attention, emotions, and actions are better off almost any way you look at it. They are happier and healthier. Their relationships are more satisfying and last longer. They make more money and go further in their careers. They are better able to manage stress, deal with conflict, and overcome adversity. They even live longer. When pit against other virtues, willpower comes out on top. Self-control is a better predictor of academic success than intelligence (take that, SATs), a stronger determinant of effective leadership than charisma (sorry, Tony Robbins), and more important for marital bliss than empathy (yes, the secret to lasting marriage may be learning how to keep your mouth shut). If we want to improve our lives, willpower is not a bad place to start."

- **Kelly McGonigal**, *The Willpower Instinct*

~~

We have said many times now that self mastery should come before material success and achievement. But if these are what you are after, self mastery still must be your starting point. With all the benefits of self mastery, it is surprising that we haven't developed a test for it and used it to replace SAT scores, IQ, and credit scores as the prime predictors of success and trustworthiness.

WIELD YOUR PASSIONS WELL

"The difference between the greatest souls and those that are base and common consists principally in the fact that common souls abandon themselves to their passions and are happy or unhappy only according as the things that happen to them are agreeable or unpleasant; the greatest souls, on the other hand, reason in a way that is so strong and cogent that, although they also have passions, and indeed passions which are often more violent than those of ordinary people, their reason nevertheless always remains mistress, and even makes their afflictions serve them and contribute to the perfect happiness they enjoy in this life."

- **René Descartes**, *Letter to Princess Elisabeth*

~~

Descartes provides a vision of the ideal being which greatly overlaps with those offered by Aristotle, Spinoza, Nietzsche, and others. It is not the absence of passion or desire which results in self mastery - this would be like driving a car with no gas. It is the ability to wield those passions to serve one's highest goals and values effectively. Strong desires can be a great thing. Having a car with a powerful engine is only a bad thing if you don't have the skill and control to wield that power without wrecking.

ADEQUATE IDEAS

"I saw that all the things I feared, and which feared me had nothing good or bad in them save insofar as the mind was affected by them."

- **Baruch Spinoza**, *Ethics*

∼

For Spinoza, the difference between freedom and bondage was the difference between adequate and inadequate ideas. When we understand that everything that happens is causally determined, we free ourselves from the blame and resentment of ourselves and others and from the anxiety of trying to control fate. When we come to see that what we view as bad is derived from our limited perspective, we can put a limit to our sadness. And when we understand that the permanence of our possessions, relationships, and souls for which we long is unattainable, we can learn to love what is permanent.

THE HAPPINESS OF MEDIOCRITY

"You are in danger of living a life so comfortable and soft, that you will die without ever realizing your true potential."

- **David Goggins**, *Can't Hurt Me*

~~

David Goggins, author of *Can't Hurt Me*, is not the first to point to the dangers of comfort, but it is always worth repeating. Do not confuse a life of comfort and ease for the good life. The good life is one of pushing your boundaries, incrementally overcoming yourself, striving for greatness - whatever that means for you. The happiness that results from the absence of discomfort is the happiness of mediocrity.

ALL-OR-NOTHING-THINKING

"Whenever you experience an unpleasant feeling or sensation, try to recall what thoughts you had been having prior to this feeling. This instruction helped them to sharpen their awareness of their thoughts, and eventually they were able to identify the thoughts prior to experiencing the emotions. Since these thoughts appeared to emerge automatically and extremely rapidly, I labeled them 'automatic thoughts'... The thoughts 'just happened,' as if by reflex. They seemed to be relatively autonomous in that the patient made no effort to initiate them and, especially in the more disturbed cases, they were difficult to 'turn off.'"

- **Aaron Beck**, *Cognitive Therapy and the Emotional Disorders*

~

When we think thoughts like "I lost my job, so I must be a total failure," we often fail to consciously think about how ridiculous the implications are. This is an example of the "All-or-Nothing Thinking" distortion: The tendency to think in extremes like "always" and "never" without considering nuanced degrees between. These thoughts happen automatically, but when we get good at identifying them, we can end their patterns and take control of our mental narratives.

DON'T IDEALIZE SUFFERING

"Strong people alone know how to organize their suffering so as to bear only the most necessary pain."

- **Emil Dorian**, *The Quality of Witness*

～

The idealization of suffering by both philosophers and popular culture has done a great disservice to people by normalizing and perpetuating experiences that would be better left behind. And the process of gradually leaving problematic emotions behind is possible for anyone with the right toolkit and commitment. Don't allow strength in one area, like rationality or creativity, allow you to justify emotional weakness.

EXPECT RESENTMENT

"When you show yourself in the world and display your talents, you naturally stir up all kinds of resentment, envy, and other manifestations of insecurity. This is to be expected. You cannot spend your life worrying about the petty feelings of others."

- **Robert Greene**, *48 Laws of Power*

~

If you ever decide to take on a bold new endeavor, don't be surprised when your friends aren't as happy for you as you expected. Most people don't want to see others, even their friends, succeed because it forces them to confront the risks they have failed to take. Expect this. But also ensure that you are not this friend. You must learn to be happy for the people close to you when they achieve or pursue something great. It means you have good influences in your life who can help lift you higher.

THE VIRTUOUS ARE FREE

"The way of the superior person is threefold; virtuous, they are free from anxieties; wise they are free from perplexities; and bold they are free from fear."

- **Confucius**, *Analects*

~

Confucius saw a world of social dissonance caused by selfishness, and believed that people needed to be molded into morally upright citizens. He thought people were overly opportunistic and driven by greed, vanity, and ignorance. They lacked respect for their families and authorities, and they did not show basic human decency for their fellow man. The person who was kind and human-hearted did the right thing for no other reason but that it was the right thing. This attitude of integrity allowed a person to realize inner serenity and equanimity, as profit and success were beside the point, and hence he could not be harmed by the lack of these things. Human flourishing was the byproduct of cultivating virtue within oneself, and of living among others who have done the same.

STOP SHOULDING YOURSELF

"Just stop doing things because you 'should.' As in, never let a 'should' feel like a reason to do something... When you're deliberating, your only responsibility is to figure out which action seems best given the available time and information."

- **Nate Soares**, *Replacing Guilt*

～

Most people feel guilty when they fail to do something they believe they 'should.' But author Nate Soares argues that this feeling of guilt is counterproductive. It often fails to push us toward our goals, and it brews bad feelings that we start to associate with the goals themselves. He says it is best to avoid the word should and simply state what will happen if we don't do the task. If there is no consequence, why do it? If there is, we will remind ourselves of the reason we want to do the task, rather than simply feeling vague obligation.

USE REALITY TO YOUR ADVANTAGE

"Our actions may be impeded, but there can be no impeding our intentions or dispositions. Because we can accommodate and adapt. The mind adapts and converts to its own purposes the obstacle to our acting. The impediment to action advances action. What stands in the way becomes the way."

- **Marcus Aurelius**, *Meditations*

~

It is crucial for our well-being that we learn to accept whatever situation we find ourselves in. But Marcus Aurelius, the great Stoic philosopher and Roman emperor, offers an advanced mindset. We can not only come to terms with difficult situations, we can learn to use them to our advantage. Your car's battery dying becomes an unexpected adventure in an otherwise boring day. A difficult transition in life becomes an opportunity to learn and grow. Don't just accept reality. Use it.

IMAGINARY PROBLEMS

"You choose to let things bother you. You can just as easily choose not to notice the irritating offender, to consider the matter trivial and unworthy of your interest. That is the powerful move. What you do not react to cannot drag you down in a futile engagement. Your pride is not involved. The best lesson you can teach an irritating gnat is to consign it to oblivion by ignoring it."

- **Robert Greene**, *48 Laws of Power*

~

Most of your problems exist only in your imagination. They are problems because you allow your mind to elevate them to problem-status. Rather than trying to solve all of your problems, see if you can simply downgrade them to non-problems and move on with your day.

DESIGN YOUR REMINDERS

"You have power over your mind — not outside events. Realize this, and you will find strength."

- **Marcus Aurelius**, *Meditations*

~

Marcus Aurelius made a regular habit of journaling his thoughts, challenges, and priorities. He had studied the work of many other Stoics who stressed that we can control only our own minds - not the outer world. But reading it and knowing it was not enough. If you don't currently have a way of journaling and writing down reminders of what is important to yourself, you will quickly forget when you come across a distraction.

THE DOCTRINE OF NONSELF

"You don't need to be accepted by others. You need to accept yourself. When you are born a lotus flower, be a beautiful lotus flower, don't try to be a magnolia flower. If you crave acceptance and recognition and try to change yourself to fit what other people want you to be, you will suffer all your life. True happiness and true power lie in understanding yourself, accepting yourself, having confidence in yourself."

- **Thich Nhat Hanh,** *The Art of Power*

~

Thich Nhat Hanh is a Vietnamese monk who practices and writes about Buddhism. One of his teachings focuses on the Buddhist doctrine of nonself, which holds that the self is an illusion. Each person is an ongoing and constantly evolving process - an aggregation of uncontrolled perceptions and cognitions. Because we believe that we each constitute a permanent and enduring self, we live selfishly, trying to accumulate and grasp onto more and more for ourselves. We want more wealth, possession, and prestige. We cling to beliefs and opinions with unwarranted certainty. This egoism leads not only to acts which harm others, but perpetuates the very cycle of suffering within ourselves. We experience anxiety, greed, and anger, the fear of all perceived threats, including our own death, all because we hold this delusion of self-hood.

LET GO OF CONTROL

"Trying to control the world?

I see you won't succeed.

The world is a spiritual vessel

And cannot be controlled.

Those who control, fail.

Those who grasp, lose.

Some go forth, some are led,

Some weep, some blow flutes,

Some become strong, some superfluous,

Some oppress, some are destroyed.

Therefore the Sage Casts off extremes,

Casts off excess,

Casts off extravagance."

- **Lao Tzu**, *Tao Te Ching*

～

In Taoism, stillness and tranquil mindfulness are the keys to shedding the layers of cultural contrivance and living only in the present moment. Everyone has within them the capacity to go beyond the individual ego and realize the boundless energy inside them. Playfulness is the appropriate attitude toward life, and every ostensible bad thing is merely a laughing matter for a Taoist sage, even death. By understanding the ways of the Tao, you can learn to be joyfully indifferent to the waves of life, and enjoy freedom and equanimity.

YOU CAN HANDLE THE TRUTH

"The strength of a person's spirit [can be] measured by how much truth he could tolerate, or more precisely, to what extent he needs to have it diluted, disguised, sweetened, muted, falsified."

- **Friedrich Nietzsche**, *Beyond Good and Evil*

~

Some people think they need certain beliefs to remain happy. That if certain cherished theories turned out to be false, they would fall into a pit of despair. But do not underestimate yourself. Not only can you handle the truth, you can learn to thrive and embrace truth for everything it is. When you accept difficult truths, you can grow to find beauty and comfort in them, and to even prefer them to the fictions. When confronting the facts, remind yourself of the resilient strength of your spirit.

LEARN AND LIVE YOUR VALUES

"Some 2,600 years ago the ancient Greek poet Pindar wrote, 'Become who you are by learning who you are.' What he meant is the following: You are born with a particular makeup and tendencies that mark you as a piece of fate. It is who you are to the core. Some people never become who they are; they stop trusting in themselves; they conform to the tastes of others, and they end up wearing a mask that hides their true nature. If you allow yourself to learn who you really are by paying attention to that voice and force within you, then you can become what you were fated to become—an individual, a Master."

- **Robert Greene**, *Mastery*

~~

Pindar, Nietzsche, Maslow, Alan Watts, and Robert Greene have all urged their readers to become who or what they are. There are clues within you that can help you actualize this potential version of yourself. Observe how you respond internally when you watch someone you admire. Watch your reaction when someone does something objectionable. Build a map of your values and shape it into a person you can strive to emulate.

BECOME FULLY HUMAN

"The goal so far as human beings are concerned - is ultimately the 'self-actualization' of a person, the becoming fully human, the development of the fullest height that the human species can stand up to or that the particular individual can come to."

- **Abraham Maslow**, *Toward a Psychology of Being*

~

Maslow was fascinated by the tiny fraction of people who seemed to embody the pinnacle of maturity and flourishing. He built a list of these great individuals, studied the qualities they all shared extensively, and constructed the concept of self-actualization from his findings. Self-actualization was the fullest manifestation of a person's inner potentialities. The imperative to self-actualize was the command to become the self which one truly is.

IMPROVEMENT OF THE SOUL

"I do nothing but go about persuading you all, old and young alike, not to take thought for your persons or properties, but first and chiefly to care about the greatest improvement of the soul."

- **Socrates**, *Plato's Apology*

~

Socrates was a Greek philosopher who lived during the 5th century BCE. He is known as the father of Western philosophy primarily due to his non-dogmatic method of questioning popular beliefs and values - a method he maintained even in the face of his own death. Socrates is also responsible for making ethics and the study of the good life topics of philosophical inquiry. Socrates is thought to have held a view on eudaimonia which blurred the lines between moral good, knowledge, and happiness. The aim of every person's life, he claimed, should be to improve his own soul or psyche, and this pursuit would result in the greatest good for all.

IMPULSES AND VALUES

"The ability to subordinate an impulse to a value is the essence of the proactive person. Reactive people are driven by feelings, by circumstances, by conditions, by their environment. Proactive people are driven by values—carefully thought about, selected and internalized values."

- **Stephen Covey**, *The 7 Habits of Highly Effective People*

~

We all face countless internal conflicts every day. To read or play video games? To exercise or stay home and eat waffles? To go out to the bar or spend time with your kids? Each of these questions represents a battle within our minds. Whether our impulses or our values win these battles determine who we will become.

BE ADDICTED TO HARD WORK

"Our culture has become hooked on the quick-fix, the life hack, efficiency. Everyone is on the hunt for that simple action algorithm that nets maximum profit with the least amount of effort. There's no denying this attitude may get you some of the trappings of success, if you're lucky, but it will not lead to a calloused mind or self-mastery. If you want to master the mind and remove your governor, you'll have to become addicted to hard work. Because passion and obsession, even talent, are only useful tools if you have the work ethic to back them up."

- **David Goggins**, *Can't Hurt Me*

~~

When you read about self development, you often find little tricks like writing in a gratitude journal or taking cold showers that will help you improve yourself. Some of these can help, but most of them are placebos that will only seem to work for a few weeks. This leaves some to write off self-improvement altogether and assume we are stuck being the same people we always were. But this couldn't be further from the truth. Changing yourself, even drastically, is possible, and David Goggins is living proof. He went from overweight and depressed to a Navy Seal and world-class endurance runner. But he didn't do it using a simple hack. The mindsets and methods matter, but none of them work without commitment and hard work

UPGRADE YOUR IDENTITY

"On any given day, you may struggle with your habits because you're too busy or too tired or too overwhelmed or hundreds of other reasons. Over the long run, however, the real reason you fail to stick with habits is that your self-image gets in the way. This is why you can't get too attached to one version of your identity. Progress requires unlearning. Becoming the best version of yourself requires you to continuously edit your beliefs, and to upgrade and expand your identity."

- **James Clear**, *Atomic Habits*

~

One of the least discussed keys to overcoming bad habits comes down to identity. Humans are built to try to preserve a positive view of themselves. Though this tendency can result in distorted self-perceptions and narcissism, it is also the key to some of the greatest human capacities. In many ways, our sense of identity shapes the actions we take and the habits we build. There is a major difference between someone who believes she is trying to learn to play the guitar and someone who believes she is a musician - someone who believes he is trying to stop drinking and someone who believes he is not a drinker.

HYPOCRITES BY DEFAULT

"Philosophy teaches us to act, not to speak; it exacts of every man that he should live according to his own standards, that his life should not be out of harmony with his words, and that, further, his inner life should be of one hue and not out of harmony with all his activities. This, I say, is the highest duty and the highest proof of wisdom—that deed and word should be in accord, that a man should be equal to himself under all conditions, and always the same."

- **Seneca**, *Letters from a Stoic*

~~~

No one likes a hypocrite - someone who preaches one thing and behaves differently. But the truth is that we are all hypocrites by default. Building a mind that is coherent and consistent all the way through is a great and difficult achievement. When anyone, including yourself, is able to act in accordance with her ideals, recognize the accomplishment for what it is.

YOUR MIND IS YOUR MASTERPIECE

"Irrigators channel waters; fletchers straighten arrows; carpenters bend wood; the wise master themselves."

- **The Buddha**, *Dhammapada*

~

The Buddha reminds us that our one true full-time job is to cultivate and master our minds. Take your psychological development into your own hands - make it your one true masterpiece. When you set your priorities this way, problems become psychological challenges - opportunities for creative improvement, rather than obstructions to happiness. Real world circumstances become a side project. External obstacles become tools for self-optimization, not problems whose conquering is an end in itself. Be the psychological equivalent of a body-builder, aiming for maximum mental fitness. The way you experience your life will change dramatically as a result.

YOU ARE IN YOUR HANDS

"Autonomous persons become fine-tuned to their own psychological well-being and inner workings. They take responsibility for regulating their thoughts, feelings and behavior."

- **Susanne Cook-Greuter**, *Nine Levels Of Increasing Embrace In Ego Development*

~

There are many people today who worked hard to get into college, took on heaps of debt to get their degree, did everything they were told to, and got out of school to find that their education had left them unprepared for the world. It is disappointing and disorienting when the institutions meant to help us end up failing us. But it is even more disappointing when no institutions even exist for helping people develop crucial life skills. Many people don't even think about the skills of self-regulation, wisdom, and well-being, specifically because they are never told to focus on these strengths. That is why, until our society steps up, it is up to each of us to carve out the path toward the peaks of psychological well-being ourselves.

DOMESTICATE YOUR DESIRES

"The chief use of wisdom lies in its teaching us to be masters of our passions and to control them with such skill that the evils which they cause are quite bearable, and even become a source of joy."

- **René Descartes**, *The Passions of the Soul*

~~

It is possible for us to regulate our desires such that we cut off our suffering when the situation calls for it. But furthermore, it is entirely possible to do this and still use them to powerfully motivate us toward rational goals. We don't need to renounce desire altogether; we just need to become proficient desire manipulators. If we can tame our desires and develop agility at modulating them so we want the right things at any given time, we can leverage them to fuel us toward our goals as effectively as possible.

ENJOY YOUR BEING

"It is an absolute perfection and virtually divine to know how to enjoy our being rightfully. We seek other conditions because we do not understand the use of our own, and go outside of ourselves because we do not know what it is like inside. Yet there is no use our mounting on stilts, for on stilts we must still walk on our own legs. And on the loftiest throne in the world we are still sitting only on our own rump."

- **Michel de Montaigne**, *The Complete Essays*

~~

Many people seek out external achievements in the name of freedom. They aim to acquire wealth so they can escape the tyranny of employment. But they end up falling into another kind of slavery to their wealth - one that creates addictions to greater and greater extrinsic rewards. They lose their ability to simply enjoy being alive. If you have the ability to love life intrinsically, recognize it as a superpower that many of the most seemingly powerful people on earth lack.

ENABLE SPONTANEITY

"The mind cannot act without giving up the impossible attempt to control itself beyond a certain point. It must let go of itself both in the sense of trusting its own memory and reflection, and in the sense of acting spontaneously, on its own into the unknown."

- **Alan Watts**, *The Way of Zen*

~~

You may think driving for self-mastery would result in a robotic existence. But this could not be further from the truth. It is by properly setting up the systems in your mind that you not only attain self-mastery, but enable yourself to act playfully and spontaneously. You don't feel the need to consciously control all your actions when you have already put the structure in place. You can stop trying so hard once you have built the right habits.

IT STARTS WITH INDIVIDUALS

"You cannot hope to build a better world without improving the individuals. To that end, each of us must work for his own improvement, and at the same time share a general responsibility for all humanity, our particular duty being to aid those to whom we think we can be most useful."

- **Marie Curie**, autobiographical notes

~~

One of the most common critiques of the pursuit of self development and self mastery is found in the claim that we should focus more on helping others or improving the world. But Marie Curie, who improved the world immensely through her pioneering research on radioactivity, argues that progress would not be possible without individual improvement. It is true that we also cannot improve the world if we all become isolated islands. But you must focus first on the smallest possible unit: yourself.

THE STAKES OF CLEAR THINKING

"The dangers of not thinking clearly are much greater now than ever before. It's not that there's something new in our way of thinking – it's that credulous and confused thinking can be much more lethal in ways it was never before."

- **Carl Sagan**, *The Demon-Haunted World*

~~

Mastering your thinking is a major part of mastering yourself because beliefs are at the root of everything else - our goals, emotions, and behaviors. But the stakes of clear thinking are higher than your own personal concerns. Irrationality, dogmatism, and ignorance are the cause of a massive proportion of global problems. Major decisions are made on the behalf of millions based on deeply flawed ideas and deliberate deception. And as technology becomes exponentially more powerful, the consequences for faulty thinking and dogmatism will rise exponentially along with it.

TURN OFF AUTOPILOT

"When you have cultivated mindfulness, life becomes richer, more vivid, more satisfying, and you don't take everything that happens so personally. Attention plays a more appropriate role within the greater context of a broad and powerful awareness. You're fully present, happier, and at ease, because you're not so easily caught up in the stories and melodramas the mind likes to concoct. Your powers of attention are used more appropriately and effectively to examine the world. You become more objective and clear-headed, and develop an enhanced awareness of the whole."

- **Culadasa**, *The Mind Illuminated*

~~

Mindfulness is a key component to a good life. Your life runs on autopilot when you aren't mindful. You miss out on the best experiences life has to offer, even when they're all around you, because you are too wrapped up in the tricks your mind plays on you. By practicing mindfulness, you unlock a new type of control that puts your satisfaction in your own hands.

THE EVER CHANGING BRAIN

"In the course of my travels I met a scientist who enabled people who had been blind since birth to begin to see, another who enabled the deaf to hear; I spoke with people who had had strokes decades before and had been declared incurable, who were helped to recover with neuroplastic treatments; I met people whose learning disorders were cured and whose IQs were raised; I saw evidence that it is possible for eighty-year-olds to sharpen their memories to function the way they did when they were fifty-five. I saw people rewire their brains with their thoughts, to cure previously incurable obsessions and traumas. I spoke with Nobel laureates who were hotly debating how we must rethink our model of the brain now that we know it is ever changing."

- **Norman Doidge**, *The Brain That Changes Itself*

~~

Neuroplasticity refers to the brain's ability to change and adapt. Your brain is changing constantly - neural pathways are being built, destroyed, and rerouted. It has become indisputable that you can change your own psychological makeup, and as a result, it is much harder to let yourself off the hook for your inadequacies. Recognize that change doesn't happen overnight. But also recognize that a failure to take on the process of change is the only thing that will ultimately prevent it from happening.

ACCEPT AND GROW

"The motivational life of self-actualizing people is not only quantitatively different but also qualitatively different from that of ordinary people. It seems probable that we must construct a profoundly different psychology of motivation for self-actualizing people, e.g., metamotivation or growth motivation, rather than deficiency motivation. Perhaps it will be useful to make a distinction between living and preparing to live. Perhaps the ordinary concept of motivation should apply only to nonself-actualizers. Our subjects no longer strive in the ordinary sense, but rather develop. They attempt to grow to perfection and to develop more and more fully in their own style. The motivation of ordinary men is a striving for the basic need gratifications that they lack. But self-actualizing people in fact lack none of these gratifications; and yet they have impulses. They work, they try, and they are ambitious, even though in an unusual sense. For them motivation is just character growth, character expression, maturation, and development; in a word self-actualization."

- **Abraham Maslow**, *Motivation and Personality*

~~

Maslow found that self-actualizers often had an unconditional acceptance of what is. The self-actualizing individual was less motivated by the need to be right or to maintain comfortable illusions, and this could allow her to perceive reality with greater clarity, detachment, and courage. She could be highly accepting of herself, including her weaknesses, and had a firm and integrated sense of identity. She could remain true to her core values and resist social pressure and enculturation. And she could accept her life circumstances, even when they were not ideal, showing great equanimity through adversity.

BEING AND HAVING

"If one feels that one's own value is not constituted primarily by the human qualities one possesses, but by one's success on a competitive market with ever-changing conditions, one's self-esteem is bound to be shaky and in constant need of confirmation by others. Hence one is driven to strive relentlessly for success, and any setback is a severe threat to one's self-esteem; helplessness, insecurity, and inferiority feelings are the result. If the vicissitudes of the market are the judges of one's value, the sense of dignity and pride is destroyed."

- **Erich Fromm**, *Man for Himself*

~

Humanistic psychologist Erich Fromm made an important distinction between being and having. If you define your self-worth by what you have, you will always be vulnerable to setbacks and loss. But if you define yourself by what you are, all of your possessions and achievements will merely be icing on the cake of your well-being. Your happiness will be on a firm foundation, and will feel more like a gradual climb as you improve than a violent roller coaster.

DEVELOPMENT OF THE SOUL

"One would have to admit that on that basis those who had been punished even more cruelly than with prison—those shot, burned at the stake—were some sort of super-evildoers. (And yet... the innocent are those who get punished most zealously of all.) And what would one then have to say about our so evident torturers: Why does not fate punish them? Why do they prosper? And the only solution to this would be that the meaning of earthly existence lies not, as we have grown used to thinking, in prospering, but... in the development of the soul. From that point of view our torturers have been punished most horribly of all: they are turning into swine, they are departing downward from humanity."

- **Aleksandr Solzhenitsyn**, *The Gulag Archipelago*

~~

Much like Viktor Frankl, Aleksandr Solzhenitsyn endured miserable conditions in a forced labor camp and wrote about his experiences. Amazingly, he actually wrote his entire book, *The Gulag Archipelago*, in his head and memorized it while in the camp, only writing it down after he was free. He argues that there is a sense in which his torturers got what they deserved. By committing horrendous acts, they corrupted their minds and became something they themselves would never approve of. We must all remember that allowing ourselves to become a person we don't love is the worst punishment in life.

YOUR OUTER WORLD SHAPES YOUR INNER WORLD

"The outer world of circumstance shapes itself to the inner world of thought, and both pleasant and unpleasant external conditions are factors which make for the ultimate good of the individual. As the reaper of his own harvest, man learns both by suffering and bliss."

- **James Allen**, *As a Man Thinketh*

~

Have you ever found yourself in a miserable job or relationship and told yourself to just toughen up? Though self mastery is our primary focus, sometimes the best option is to leave an environment that is holding us back. An unpleasant environment will place unpleasant thoughts into your mind and make your life much harder. Surround yourself with people who have priorities, traits, or practices you would like to cultivate in yourself, and leave the rest behind.

WAKE UP AND BECOME

"It is time for man to fix his goal. It is time for man to plant the seed of his highest hope. His soil is still rich enough for it. But this soil will one day be poor and weak; no longer will a high tree be able to grow from it. Alas! The time is coming when man will no more shoot the arrow of his longing out over mankind, and the string of his bow will have forgotten how to twang! I tell you: one must have chaos in one, to give birth to a dancing star. I tell you: you still have chaos in you."

- **Friedrich Nietzsche**, *Thus Spoke Zarathustra*

～～

Nietzsche believed that the culture of his day produced people who were complacent consumers, happy to remain in a dull nest of comfort their whole lives. It made them feel guilty about their drives toward creative aspiration and growth and numbed them into lives of shallow pleasure and sluggishness. But he tried his best to inspire a few to wake up to the chaos inside them and strive toward greatness. To turn away from the herd of mediocrity and define their own lives. Don't simply be, Nietzsche would say. Become.

THE POWER OF INDIFFERENCE

"Demand not that events should happen as you wish; but wish them to happen as they do happen, and your life will be serene."

- **Epictetus**, *Enchiridion*

~

A good Stoic should refrain from any qualitative judgment of an event or circumstance and view it with total objectivity. Everything from good fortune, to insult, to our closest relationships should all be viewed with indifference. In order to achieve this objective tranquility, the Stoics engaged in mental exercises, such as reflecting on the possibility of loss as a way of curbing expectations. Though seemingly harsh, you can use this philosophy to take an attitude of radical acceptance of everything that happens to you. This will allow you to remain happy, even when your circumstances are ostensibly bad.

THE GARDEN OF THE MIND

"A man's mind may be likened to a garden, which may be intelligently cultivated or allowed to run wild; but whether cultivated or neglected, it must, and will, bring forth. If no useful seeds are put into it, then an abundance of useless weed seeds will fall therein, and will continue to produce their kind."

- **James Allen**, *As a Man Thinketh*

~~

What you feed your mind is what you will become. If all you feed it is episodes of *The Bachelor*, don't expect it to be any deeper than your glass of champaign. If all you do is work, don't expect to be fun to be around. Once you identify what your ideal self looks like, the next question to ask is what balance of lifestyle will bring you closer to it in all the important ways.

WHAT ELEVATES YOUR SOUL?

"Let the youthful soul look back on life with the question: what have you truly loved up to now, what has elevated your soul, what has mastered it and at the same time delighted it? Place these venerated objects before you in a row, and perhaps they will yield for you, through their nature and their sequence, a law, the fundamental law of your true self."

- **Friedrich Nietzsche**, *Schopenhauer as Educator*

~

Nietzsche believed that virtue was unique to each person, and the pursuit of the good life was an individualistic endeavor. The great individual takes on a project of discovery and experimentation for determining what was good for him. And he suggests that this journey can be guided by asking yourself what you feel has elevated and delighted your soul. He viewed the will to power, or the drive to increase your power in all possible forms, as the fundamental driving force of life. To fail to expand your individual powers was to reject the very force of life. So experiment and learn what makes you feel empowered and alive, and seek more of it.

BE GROUNDED IN THE PRESENT

"To dwell in the here and now does not mean you never think about the past or responsibly plan for the future. The idea is simply not to allow yourself to get lost in regrets about the past or worries about the future. If you are firmly grounded in the present moment, the past can be an object of inquiry, the object of your mindfulness and concentration. You can attain many insights by looking into the past. But you are still grounded in the present moment."

- **Thich Nhat Hanh**, *The Art of Power*

~~

Many people assume that the ideal enlightened monk would spend no time thinking about the past or the future. If this were the goal, it could be achieved much more quickly with a frontal lobotomy. By learning to live in the present, you free yourself from rumination and worry, but not from the ability to plan or solve problems. Thinking becomes a tool you can use at will rather than a compulsion.

THE VOYAGE OF LIFE

"You may not control all the events that happen to you, but you can decide not to be reduced by them. Try to be a rainbow in someone's cloud. Do not complain. Make every effort to change things you do not like. If you cannot make a change, change the way you have been thinking. You might find a new solution."

- **Maya Angelou**, *Letter to My Daughter*

~

Life can be compared to a voyage. There is no chance you will sail through life without having to endure storms at some point - trying to steer your ship around the storms is futile. So instead, try to build up your boat to be so robust and strong that the storms can't break it. Before you know it, your tiny canoe will have transformed into a towering cruise liner. You can stand on the deck and look out over the vast ocean, surrounded by people still floundering in feeble canoes. The same waves that send others flying into the sea will be nothing more than a gentle rocking for you.

WISDOM IS A SKILL

"We start trying to be wise when we realize that we are not born knowing how to live, but that life is a skill that has to be acquired, like learning to ride a bicycle or play the piano."

- **Alain de Botton**, *On Love*

~~

Contrary to popular belief, wisdom does not always come with age. It comes with the obsessive desire to acquire it. The wise have carefully observed and learned of the pitfalls of emotional prediction. They have developed an understanding of their own well-being trajectory, and learned, from their own experience, that of others, or reflection, that the thing which seems like the best idea can be illusory. They have identified counter-intuitive practical truths, and crucially, make the decision to listen to them rather than making the same mistakes when they know better.

THE GIFT OF TROUBLEMAKERS

"Hard times build determination and inner strength. Through them we can also come to appreciate the uselessness of anger. Instead of getting angry, nurture a deep caring and respect for troublemakers because by creating such trying circumstances they provide us with invaluable opportunities to practice tolerance and patience."

- **Dalai Lama XIV**, *How to Practice*

~~

The Dalai Lama is one of the greatest living spiritual teachers, but his ideas are not advanced. They are incredibly simple - they are just so hard to put into practice. But they are not impossible if you make them a priority. Before you start your next day, tell yourself (ideally out loud) that you will be thankful for the troublemakers and annoyances you will encounter today. Be grateful for the opportunity to cultivate greater self mastery.

LIMIT YOUR WORRIES

"If the problem can be solved why worry? If the problem cannot be solved worrying will do you no good."

- **Shantideva**, *Guide to the Bodhisattva's Way of Life*

～

Worry likely exists as a mechanism to make sure we are prepared for the important moments in our lives. Someone who didn't worry at all might float through life without ever doing anything meaningful. So rather than trying to get rid of worry altogether, try this: Allow yourself a designated period of time (could be daily or weekly) to worry. Let yourself consider all the worst possibilities and nightmare scenarios to get it out of your system. When the period is up, remind yourself that the worry has done its job and is no longer needed.

PRACTICE ASCETICISM

"I am so firmly determined, however, to test the constancy of your mind that, drawing from the teachings of great men, I shall give you also a lesson: Set aside a certain number of days, during which you shall be content with the scantiest and cheapest fare, with coarse and rough dress, saying to yourself the while: 'Is this the condition that I feared?'"

- **Seneca**, *Letters from a Stoic*

~

If you find that certain dependencies are causing you to act against your goals, you can use the practice of asceticism, or voluntary discomfort, to intentionally deprive yourself of some desired and attainable object. The practice has been used by some to serve as self-punishment, which has led some to quickly write it off. But the useful purpose of asceticism is to break dependencies and make yourself more emotionally robust. Asceticism can be used to weaken a desire's hold on you and break the soft addictions that lock you into bad habits.

HOLDING ON WILL HOLD YOU BACK

"See them, floundering in their sense of mine, like fish in the puddles of a dried-up stream — and, seeing this, live with no mine, not forming attachment for states of becoming."

- **The Buddha**, *Sutta Nipata*

~~

Buddhism talks a lot about the problems with attachment. But the point is not to be completely indifferent to everything or to forgo secure, interpersonal relationships. Non-attachment and embrace are all about your mental orientation to the goals, objects, and relationships in your life. You have the choice to reject the fantasies of total control and permanence. You can turn your circumstances into your playground. You can opt out of the game everyone else is playing, and play a better game.

ORDER FROM WITHIN

"The person who is developing freely and naturally arrives at a spiritual equilibrium in which he is master of his actions, just as one who has acquired physical poise can move freely. When he is master of himself he is also flexible in his attitude toward others, and capable of adaptation to the wishes and requirements of others... Hitherto man has connected the word 'discipline' with the idea of mastery by someone else... But this is not so. When the order is not imposed from without, but formed naturally from within, discipline and liberty are identical. As the soul of man advances in this inner discipline, so much the freer it is to develop and expand."

- **Maria Montessori**, Lecture at Central Hall, Westminster

~~

One of the lesser known thinkers on human growth and potential was Maria Montessori, creator of the Montessori educational philosophy. The Montessori method is unique in its attempt to help children grow and learn naturally through play and hands-on exploration. Though it was, and still is commonly believed that children must be forced to work and learn, Montessori argued that the sooner a person is allowed to direct their own course, the more naturally he will acquire autonomy and self-discipline. Self mastery begins at an early age, so take every opportunity to let young people strengthen their own self-direction capacities.

INTRINSIC MOTIVATION

"Just as a solid rock is not shaken by the storm, even so the wise are not affected by praise or blame."

- **The Buddha**, *Dhammapada*

~

If you find that you require constant praise to stay motivated, consider the nature of those motivations. Numerous studies have shown that intrinsic motivation, which consists of doing things we find enjoyable and engaging, can be more powerful than extrinsic rewards like praise. It can be far more effective to choose goals which we already have strong desires pushing us toward than to reward ourselves for going against our desires. But counterintuitively, the overwhelming evidence suggests that extrinsic rewards can not only be weakly motivating, but can actually hurt our motivation and yield inferior work than intrinsic drive.

PLANT SEEDS FOR YOUR MIND

"You shape the garden of your mind by planting specific things from your environment, such as the books you read, experiences you have, and people you surround yourself with."

- **Benjamin Hardy**, *Willpower Doesn't Work*

~~

L ook around at how your living space is arranged. What behaviors does it promote and what does it neglect or discourage? Would you say the physical space you spend your time in is representative of the person you would like to be? Your digital environments shape you as well. The websites you visit regularly, the podcasts you subscribe to, and the apps you keep on your phone will shape you. If you want to be less distracted, disable the notifications and unsubscribe from the email newsletters that you don't feel push you in the direction of your ideals, and consider subscribing those that do.

BECOME EMOTIONALLY INVINCIBLE

"Be like a headland of rock on which the waves break incessantly; but it stands fast and around it the seething of the waters sink to rest."

- **Marcus Aurelius**, *Meditations*

~~

Imagine how much fun it would to be physically invincible. To enter a sword-fight unarmed and to exit without a scratch, leaving your opponent frustrated and exhausted. When you become emotionally invincible, your opponent may be another person shelling out insults, your own inner critic, or simply the unexpected blows life deals to us all. These petty attempts to break you will begin to amuse you more than they dishearten you once you learn their game. Whether you are forced to suffer over the blows or laugh at them is all a matter of how developed your cognitive toolkit is.

THE SUCCESS NARRATIVE

"Listen to what is being preached today. Look at everyone around us. You've wondered why they suffer, why they seek happiness and never find it. If any man stopped and asked himself whether he's ever held a truly personal desire, he'd find the answer. He'd see that all his wishes, his efforts, his dreams, his ambitions are motivated by other men. He's not really struggling even for material wealth, but for the second-hander's delusion - prestige. A stamp of approval, not his own. He can find no joy in the struggle and no joy when he has succeeded. He can't say about a single thing: 'This is what I wanted because I wanted it, not because it made my neighbors gape at me'. Then he wonders why he's unhappy."

- **Ayn Rand**, *The Fountainhead*

~~

We naturally acquire beliefs about which goals are worth striving for from our culture, and every culture has its own "success" narrative. This narrative assigns arbitrary milestones that deem people "successful" after they meet them. These milestones are not necessarily to be avoided. Being an unconditional nonconformist is nothing to be proud of. It is inevitable that the goals you set for yourself will mesh with cultural prescription from time to time. But don't do them out of blind conformity to a social script. Achieving goals is not enough to bring satisfaction - they must be in line with your inner nature.

CELEBRATE THE END

"The world is afflicted by death and decay. But the wise do not grieve, having realized the nature of the world."

- **The Buddha**, *Sutta Nipata*

~

Buddhism encourages people to develop a different kind of relationship with their gains, possessions, and even their loved ones. When we fully understand that all things must end, we can learn to appreciate the finite amount of time we have with others and celebrate the end rather than repeatedly mourning the tragedy of impermanence. By comprehending the inevitability of death and loss, we can learn to experience grief to the right degree and duration instead of resigning to it.

SELF-OPTIMIZE OBSESSIVELY

"When we learn, we alter which genes in our neurons are "expressed," or turned on. Our genes have two functions. The first, the "template function," allows our genes to replicate, making copies of themselves that are passed from generation to generation. The template function is beyond our control. The second is the "transcription function." Each cell in our body contains all our genes, but not all those genes are turned on, or expressed. When a gene is turned on, it makes a new protein that alters the structure and function of the cell... Thus we can shape our genes, which in turn shape our brain's microscopic anatomy."

- **Norman Doidge**, *The Brain That Changes Itself*

~

The modern fascination with neuroplasticity has led many to try to optimize their intelligence, memory, and concentration. People obsessively track and optimize their sleep, nutrition, and exercise regimens. But people who obsessively and directly optimize the structure of their minds for flourishing are less common. It is literally possible to alter your own gene expression through learning, practice, and conditioning. Don't miss a single day's opportunity to decide what kind of machine your brain will be.

COMFORT IS AN ADDICTION

"We love comfort. We love state-of-the-art practice facilities, oak-paneled corner offices, spotless locker rooms, and fluffy towels. Which is a shame, because luxury is a motivational narcotic: It signals our unconscious minds to give less effort. It whispers, Relax, you've made it."

- **Daniel Coyle**, *The Little Book of Talent*

~~

The most obvious examples of addiction are the chemicals that form physical dependencies. Synthetic drugs like cocaine tap directly into our brain's reward circuits. But the things we are used to calling addictions are not the only type of modern pleasures that continually hold people back. Ultimately, an addiction is any maladaptive behavior which controls an individual rather than being controlled by him. Too much comfort can preclude adaptive behaviors, limiting people from building healthy lives and relationships and obstructing the value alignment that would result in genuine satisfaction. Ensure that you keep some amount of discomfort in your life to keep yourself from stagnating.

SORT OUT YOUR INTUITIONS

"Your time is limited, so don't waste it living someone else's life. Don't be trapped by dogma—which is living with the results of other people's thinking. Don't let the noise of others' opinions drown out your own inner voice. And most important, have the courage to follow your heart and intuition. They somehow already know what you truly want to become. Everything else is secondary."

- **Steve Jobs**, Stanford University Commencement Speech

~~

How do we actually get in touch with our intuitions? Should we follow our hearts, truth, bliss, or some other vague idea? Start by making a list of the people you most admire and be specific about the things you admire them for. Group them into six to twelve categories and assign labels to them. When you feel that you have finished, ask yourself what kind of life would allow you to embody these qualities, and start taking the first steps to living it.

THE OPPORTUNITY IN TRAGEDY

"There are heights of the soul from which even tragedy ceases to look tragic."

- **Friedrich Nietzsche**, *Beyond Good and Evil*

~

The point of this quote is not that we should celebrate diseases, natural disasters, or other tragedies. The point is that it is possible to reach a state in which you no longer see failure or defeat in your life as a tragedy. Once you have experienced enough of it, you will begin to view these stumbling blocks as the mountains that most need to be climbed. Ask how the tragedy could be an opportunity.

EMOTIONAL CONSEQUENCES

"The demarcation between a positive and a negative desire or action is not whether it gives you an immediate feeling of satisfaction but whether it ultimately results in positive or negative consequences."

- **Dalai Lama XIV**, *The Art of Happiness*

~

Wisdom allows you to understand that investing in your education is probably a better means to becoming a billionaire than investing in lottery tickets. But even more crucially, wisdom allows you to question whether becoming a billionaire is a worthy end in the first place. The heart of the pursuit of wisdom is that you can be easily deceived about your own well-being.

PROPER BALANCE

"The just man will not allow the three elements [reason, spirit, desire] which make up his inward self to trespass on each other's functions or interfere with each other, but by keeping all three in tune, like the notes of a scale... will in the truest sense set his house in order, and be his own lord and master, and at peace with himself. When he has bound these elements into a single controlled and orderly whole, and so unified himself, he will be ready for action of any kind."

- **Plato**, *The Republic*

~

Plato argued that a person was like a charioteer, and reason, our irrational impulses, and emotions were the horses which pulled in often conflicting directions. Desire for wealth may pull an individual in one direction, and the desire for social status may pull in another. Bodily impulses for food and sex may pull in other directions still. All parts had to be kept in proper balance - trained, so the soul did not become ruled by any passion disproportionately. Are your reason, desires, and emotions in proper balance, or does one dominate over the others?

CONTROL YOUR IMPRESSIONS

"I should never think of any external event, or any impression that follows from an external event, as forcing me to consider it in one way or in another. The mind is not passively moved about by objects, but is rather an active principle that forms a conscious awareness of those objects. I can react in my own way, based upon my own judgment, and there is the good and the bad in it relative to me. There is a liberation from the burden of conditions here, an embrace of true freedom in the face of outside forces."

- **Marcus Aurelius**, *Meditations*

~

The Stoics were all about finding methods for controlling their own impressions. Take the incredibly simple practice of gratitude. Gratitude can be used as a method for increasing all desires for what you already have. It is an excellent strategy for countering the disappointment of failure by shifting emotional investment away from new gains and toward things that you already have, such as loved ones, achievements, or fortunate living conditions. Often the greatest barrier to serenity is too many desires for what we don't possess and too few for what we do. So when you lose something, take control of your own impressions and be grateful for the things you still have.

THE GOLDEN MEAN

"Again, the work of man is achieved only in accordance with practical wisdom as well as with moral virtue; for virtue makes us aim at the right mark, and practical wisdom makes us take the right means."

- **Aristotle**, *Nicomachean Ethics*

~

According to Aristotle, the ideal balance of the passions was defined as a mean between two extremes, and this mean varied by circumstance. Courage was the ideal mean between cowardice and rashness, and pride between humility and vanity. In this sense, ethics could be compared to aesthetics, striving toward beauty, proportion, and harmony. Determining the "golden mean" was a job for reason and practical wisdom, and a good person had to excel in rational inquiry, introspection, and deliberation in order to properly evaluate it.

STEP OFF OF THE TREADMILL

"Do not spoil what you have by desiring what you have not; remember that what you now have was once among the things you only hoped for."

- **Epicurus**, *Principal Doctrines*

~~

Envy is the feeling which results from comparing oneself to another and finding that they have something we want or feel we deserve. We experience envy to drive us to fight for more wealth, higher status, and more sexual partners. But when we envy someone, we deprive ourself of the satisfaction of appreciating what we have and keep ourselves on the vicious treadmill of gain which will never deliver satisfaction. Envy and comparison can prevent our satisfaction from ever increasing, regardless of how high our living standard rises. In order to fight it, we have to embed what is important to us into our minds, and what is important should never be relative to those around us.

REINFORCE YOUR IDENTITY

"The effect of one-off experiences tends to fade away while the effect of habits gets reinforced with time, which means your habits contribute most of the evidence that shapes your identity. In this way, the process of building habits is actually the process of becoming yourself."

- **James Clear**, *Atomic Habits*

~~

Our habits serve as evidence of the type of person we are to ourselves which in turn adds fuel to the habits themselves. If we do nothing, we have no evidence of the type of person we are. And if we consistently do all the things our ideal self would, we have all the evidence we need. Our behaviors are the constant neuroplastic reinforcement that program our mind. So unless we take an active role in this programming, who we are and how closely we align with our ideals will be purely a consequence of chance.

INCREASE YOUR POWER

"But the objects of our passions, being external to us, are completely beyond our control. Thus, the more we allow ourselves to be controlled by them, the more we are subject to passions and the less active and free we are."

- **Baruch Spinoza**, *Ethics*

~~

All beings, Spinoza thought, strive to preserve themselves and increase their power to do so. This power was the foundation of virtue, and every impulse we experience was developed by nature for this purpose. Joy, love, and hope are all related to the increase of our power to persevere, and sadness, hate, and fear are all related to a decrease in this power. But when anything external to our nature is able to increase or decrease this power, it puts us in bondage. Our well-being becomes fully at the whim of the world, which will beat us around like waves in the sea.

ANGER IS A TEST

"The greatest remedy for anger is delay: beg anger to grant you this at the first, not in order that it may pardon the offense, but that it may form a right judgment about it - if it delays, it will come to an end. Do not attempt to quell it all at once, for its first impulses are fierce; by plucking away its parts we shall remove the whole... In the lowest recess of the heart let it be hidden away, and let it not drive, but be driven. Moreover, let us change all its symptoms into the opposite: let the expression on our faces be relaxed, our voices gentler, our steps more measured; little by little outer features mold inner ones."

- **Seneca**, *On Anger*

~

Here he proposes a counter to anger that involves simply delaying our reactions, gradually chipping away at our impulses of rage until we can think clearly. He suggests that by controlling our expressions of anger, we can keep it contained, prevent it from doing any damage, and train our inner feelings of anger to mirror our outer expressions of equanimity. If we can build habits like these to be triggered automatically by feelings of anger, we can gradually master the emotion. Learn to view every frustration you encounter as a test of mental strength, and you will get better and better at maintaining your patience, levity, and control.

INSIGHTFUL AMBIGUITY

"The whole process of nature is an integrated process of immense complexity, and it's really impossible to tell whether anything that happens in it is good or bad — because you never know what will be the consequence of the misfortune; or, you never know what will be the consequences of good fortune."

- **Alan Watts**, *Swimming Headless*

~

We often look back on past events and see that everything worked out in the end. We see that the things we thought were so terrible at the time actually ended up being good for us in the long run. But almost no one talks about their lives in the moment with this type of insightful ambiguity. We are always sure of what is desirable or undesirable at the time. We insist on chasing what we want, oversimplifying the complex mechanics of the world to an absurd degree. Relying on our internal life-simulator to guide us through life is like relying on a child's crayon map to guide us through New York City.

THE BEGINNER MINDSET

"The problem with all students... they hear an idea and they hold on to it until it becomes dead; they want to flatter themselves that they know the truth. But true Zen never stops, never congeals into such truths. That is why everyone must constantly be pushed to the abyss, starting over and feeling their utter worthlessness as a student. Without suffering and doubts, the mind will come to rest on clichés and stay there, until the spirit dies as well. Not even enlightenment is enough. You must continually start over and challenge yourself."

- **Robert Greene**, *Mastery*

~

If you want to learn to play an instrument, the second best time to start is now. The best time to start would have been when you were four years old. But it isn't just because your brain was still so malleable at that age. It's because young kids don't struggle with their egos as much as adults do when learning something new. Everything is new for them, so they are used to being pushed into new territory and not being an expert. As soon as you get a taste of knowing what you're doing, being good at things, and having it all figured out, you can't let it go. But we can learn from this beginner's mindset. We can push ourselves into uncomfortable area of non-expertise and remember that the goal is to learn, not to know.

ACT AS IF THE WORLD WERE WATCHING

"Whenever you do a thing, though it can be known but to yourself, ask yourself how you would act were all the world looking at you, and act accordingly. Encourage all your virtuous dispositions, and exercise them whenever an opportunity arises; being assured that they will gain strength by exercise, as a limb of the body does, and that exercise will make them habitual."

- **Thomas Jefferson**, Letter to Peter Carr

~~

Other people's opinions may not be the ones that matter, but they can be a powerful tool to shape ourselves. Like it or not, we all care about what other people think. So whenever you do something, pretend all of the people you admire most are watching. This will help remind you of your priorities and hold you accountable for them.

DON'T AVOID DISCOMFORT

"Nothing in the world is worth having or worth doing unless it means effort, pain, difficulty... I have never in my life envied a human being who led an easy life. I have envied a great many people who led difficult lives and led them well."

- **Theodore Roosevelt**, *American Ideals*

~~

You cannot build a robust mind by sheltering yourself from difficulty. Avoiding uncomfortable surroundings will make you vulnerable when things don't go according to plan. Avoiding uncomfortable feedback will keep you from developing your ideas and developing into the person you are capable of being. Avoiding uncomfortable beliefs will shield you from the truth. And avoiding uncomfortable situations will create barriers which may keep you from ever knowing who you were capable of being. You must learn to do what scares you.

DEATH IS NOTHING TO US

"Death is nothing to us; for the body, when it has been resolved into its elements, has no feeling, and that which has no feeling is nothing to us."

- **Epicurus**, *Principal Doctrines*

~~

How much time do you spend contemplating or worrying about death? Epicurus thought the fear of death was the chief disturbance of the mind. In the attempt to extinguish this fear, he argued that the belief that death was a threat to the individual was at odds with reason and an accurate understanding of nature. Some people seem to imagine death as being trapped in a coffin for eternity, and it's no wonder they dread it so much. Epicurus reminds us that death is not an experience any of us will actually have because we will no longer be experiencing anything by the time we are gone, so it shouldn't be cause for concern.

BE YOUR OWN SCULPTOR

"Any man could, if he were so inclined, be the sculptor of his own brain."

- **Santiago Ramon y Cajal**, *Advice for a Young Investigator*

~~

Neuroplasticity gives us the ability to gradually improve at things through consistent and sustained effort. And mastery is a relative term which does not indicate that one can reach a point at which no further progress can be made. By becoming intimately aware of the mistakes that we would like to relinquish - by working out the disadvantageous habits and building advantageous ones, we can develop the ability to increasingly determine our own subjective experience.

CREATE YOURSELF

"Engaged in the creative process we feel more alive than ever, because we are making something and not merely consuming, Masters of the small reality we create. In doing this work, we are in fact creating ourselves."

- **Robert Greene**, *Mastery*

~

C ontrary to popular belief, creativity isn't this thing that happens in an art class. Being creative isn't some niche for a small group of people. Creativity is behind a drive at the core of all humans - to exert control over your environment. To express and bring out into the world what is at your core. If you believe you are not a creative person, it means you are the product of a culture which has suppressed your creativity. It's possible that some people won't be inclined to paint or make music. But it isn't possible to be a person and not be creative. Not being creative would mean not having anything going on inside you which could be expressed. To be an empty shell. You may not have learned how see or express what is inside you, but this is a matter of alterable learning and suppression - not innate ability.

THE HARMONIOUS GROUND OF BEING

"Lack of power to moderate and restrain the affects I call Bondage. For the man who is subject to affects is under the control, not of himself, but of fortune, in whose power he so greatly is that often, though he sees the better for himself, he is still forced to follow the worse."

- **Baruch Spinoza**, *Ethics*

~

For Spinoza, the great solution to our passionate suffering and bondage was to increase our intellectual knowledge, and love, for eternal nature. The degree to which we could understand this great harmonious ground of being was the degree of equanimity, calmness, and self-control we could attain. And in realizing the union of all, we could come to feel more connected and benevolent toward others, wanting for everyone else whatever we want for ourselves. When we develop a clear and distinct understanding of these truths, our view of the world comes to resemble the mind of God.

SAY YES TO LIFE

"I have often asked myself whether I am not much more deeply indebted to the hardest years of my life than to any others. According to the voice of my innermost nature, everything necessary, seen from above and in the light of a superior economy, is also useful in itself—not only should one bear it, one should love it... Amor fati: this is the very core of my being—And as to my prolonged illness, do I not owe much more to it than I owe to my health? To it I owe a higher kind of health, a sort of health which grows stronger under everything that does not actually kill it!—To it, I owe even my philosophy... it forces us philosophers to descend into our nethermost depths, and to let go of all trustfulness, all good-nature, all whittling-down, all mildness, all mediocrity,—on which things we had formerly staked our humanity. I doubt whether such suffering improves a man; but I know that it makes him deeper... One is another person when one leaves these protracted and dangerous exercises in the art of self-mastery."

- **Friedrich Nietzsche**, *The Case of Wagner*

~~~

In contrast with the life-denying spirit Nietzsche thought pervaded the ethics of many modern religions, the great life was one characterized by affirmation. It is possible and desirable for you to learn to truly love life, not just the seemingly pleasant parts of it. You can live cheerfully even while enduring adversity and pain, and embrace who you are with unapologetic pride. You can say "yes" to life, even to the point of willing that you should relive it the exact same way for all of eternity.

ANGER HARMS YOU FIRST

"Surely every man will want to restrain any impulse towards anger when he realizes that it begins by inflicting harm, firstly, on himself! In the case of those who give full rein to anger and consider it a proof of strength, who think the opportunity for revenge belongs among the great blessings of great fortune, do you not, then, want me to point out to them that a man who is the prisoner of his own anger, so far from being powerful, cannot even be called free?"

- **Seneca**, *On Anger*

~~

Anger arises when you perceive that your strategic goals have been impeded through the fault of someone else. But most of the time, our anger is directed toward situations or inanimate objects. It is only after we remind ourselves that there is no conscious target of blame that our anger subsides, and it becomes clear that our rage and hatred has caused no one pain but ourselves. As one understands the true causes and motives of his enemy's actions, assigning blame for anything becomes less and less reasonable. Great people develop superior strategies for dealing with obstacles, threats, and aggression. A person who can stand her ground while responding to aggressors with compassion, humor, and reasonable consideration will win more battles than one who goes into a rage.

RELINQUISH CERTAINTY

"Not-knowing is true knowledge.

Presuming to know is a disease.

First realize that you are sick;

Then you can move toward health.

The Master is her own physician.

She has healed herself of all knowing.

Thus she is truly whole."

- **Lao Tzu**, *Tao Te Ching*

~

When we think we know something, we prevent ourselves from learning more or considering alternative possibilities. If you want to get closer to true knowledge, notice which ideas you are attached to and which ones you resist. The areas you tend to turn your curiosity away from - that make you defensive when they are called into question. Perhaps you feel highly resistant to questioning a certain belief because you are a part of a group which is based on that belief. Or maybe you feel like one belief provides you with a critical coping mechanism - one that you would be lost without. Write these observations down.

WILL ONE THING

"The first condition for more than mediocre achievement in any field, including that of the art of living, is to will one thing. To will one thing presupposes having made a decision, having committed oneself to one goal. It means that the whole person is geared and devoted to the one thing he has decided on, that all his energies flow in the direction of this chosen goal. Where energies are split in different directions, an aim is not only striven for with diminished energy, but the split of energies has the effect of weakening them in both directions by the constant conflicts that are engendered."

- **Erich Fromm**, *The Art of Being*

~

Have you decided what you really want? If you want to be the CEO of a billion dollar business and also want to spend every day relaxing on the beach, chances are you won't be able to achieve either one. The power of choosing a single-pointed goal is hard to overstate, as failing to choose is one of the most common reasons people get nowhere. If you want to do everything, don't be surprised to find yourself stuck and unable to do anything.

DON'T FIND YOUR TRUE SELF - BUILD IT

"It is a myth to believe that we will find our authentic self after we have left behind or forgotten one thing or another... To make ourselves, to shape a form from various elements – that is the task! The task of a sculptor! Of a productive human being!"

- **Friedrich Nietzsche**, unpublished notes

~~

There is lots of talk today about discovering your true self or finding your passion. All this implies that self-discovery can be a passive process of waiting until your true self comes along and smacks you in the face. But Nietzsche reminds us that you will never find this authentic self if you sit around waiting for it. You don't find yourself - you have to create it. You don't discover your passion - you build it. If you want to live an authentic life, start taking action, conduct experiments, and see what sticks.

APPROPRIATE EMOTIONS

"Anybody can become angry - that is easy, but to be angry with the right person and to the right degree and at the right time and for the right purpose, and in the right way - that is not within everybody's power and is not easy."

- **Aristotle**, *Nicomachean Ethics*

~

Aristotle proposed the notion that we should strive not to remove all negative emotion, but to experience appropriate emotions in appropriate proportions. This can be refreshing to hear for those who feel like they are doing something wrong every time they have a slightly unpleasant emotion. Which emotions do you want to feel? Would your ideal self get angry over being disrespected, or simply laugh it off and deal with it as necessary? Would your ideal self be perfectly tranquil at your parent's funeral, or would you grieve for a period of time? Which reaction is most conducive to your goals? You must answer each of these questions for yourself.

GRADE YOURSELF PROPERLY

"Remember too on every occasion which leads thee to vexation to apply this principle: not that this is a misfortune, but that to bear it nobly is good fortune."

- **Marcus Aurelius**, *Meditations*

~

So many people are too hard on themselves because they grade themselves on where they end up in their lives. But you can make things much better for yourself by shifting the way you measure your life. When you fail to get a job you were hoping for, don't give yourself a bad 'score' for not getting the job. Give yourself a bad score if you handle the news poorly. Give yourself a ten out of ten if you accept the news, try to learn from this experience, move on to the next opportunity, and improve wherever necessary.

YOU ARE NOT HELPLESS

"Man has the key to understanding and solving his psychological disturbance within the scope of his own awareness. He can correct the misconceptions producing his emotional disturbance with the same problem-solving apparatus that he has been accustomed to using at various stages of his development."

- **Aaron Beck**, *Cognitive Therapy and the Emotional Disorders*

~~

Aaron Beck observed that all of the main psychotherapeutic methods of his day, from the psychoanalytic to the behavioral, shared the assumption that neuroses arise through impenetrable forces outside of the individual's awareness or control. Whether these forces were of chemical or historical origin, they required a trained healer to resolve. The idea he introduced to psychotherapy was incredibly empowering. Each of us has everything we need to correct our problematic emotions. This does not mean we can't seek help from others. It simply means we are not helpless to change ourselves.

ELIMINATE COMPLICATION

"We must sacrifice many things to which we are addicted, thinking them to be goods. Gone is courage, which should be continually testing itself; gone is greatness of soul, which cannot stand out clearly unless it has learned to scorn as trivial everything that the crowd covets as supremely important."

- **Seneca**, *Letters from a Stoic*

~

If it is pleasure you crave, you can temporarily deprive yourself of food (fasting), sex, or a drug to weaken the desire. Minor acts of social sacrifice, such as neglecting an opportunity to signal something positive about yourself, can decrease your desire for status, approval, and validation. And giving away all but the most necessary possessions in the spirit of minimalism can limit the innate desire to accumulate and horde. You can even take this ascetic spirit to an extreme by completely renouncing some forms of desire. You can refuse to accumulate new toys. Reject all social media platforms. Commit to give away all of your money once you have achieved a sustainable lifestyle. For every type of perpetual desire you are able to renounce, you remove complication from your life.

THE COURAGE TO QUESTION

"Is it really so difficult simply to accept as true everything we have been taught, and which has gradually taken firm root in us, and is thought true by the circle of our relatives and many good people, and which, moreover, really does comfort and elevate men? Is that more difficult than to venture on new paths, at odds with custom, in the insecurity that attends independence, experiencing many mood-swings and even troubles of conscience, often disconsolate, but always with the true, the beautiful and the good as our goal?... Every true faith is infallible, it accomplishes what the person holding the faith hopes to find in it, but that does not offer the slightest support for a proof of its objective truth. Here the ways of men divide: if you wish to strive for peace of soul and happiness, then believe; if you wish to be a disciple of truth, then inquire."

- **Friedrich Nietzsche**, letter to his sister, Elizabeth

~

When you hear someone express a view that clashes with yours, your instinct will be to get defensive. This person will instantly become your enemy, and your goal will be to prove how ignorant and stupid their ideas are. When you start to feel this way, pause, and give this person some credit for going against the grain. It takes courage to question popular ideas, so even if you still end up disagreeing with them, recognize that they are doing something admirable. You must come to pride yourself, not on the accuracy of your current beliefs, but on your willingness to abandon your beliefs for new, more accurate ones.

THE PATH OF SELF MASTERY

"A disciplined mind brings happiness."

- **The Buddha**, *Dhammapada*

~~

The Buddha didn't just praise self mastery, he offered actionable steps to work toward it. One component consisted in ethical behavior, which involved treating other people compassionately in one's actions and speech, and refraining from a list of unethical acts like murder and theft. A second component was mental discipline, which entailed the cultivation of wholesome mental states, and the diligent practice of exercises for cultivating mindfulness. The primary mindfulness exercise was vipassana meditation, which aimed to train the mind through a single-pointed and non-attached awareness of one's own ever-changing field of consciousness. The final factor of the path was wisdom, which entailed seeking to transcend one's ego and the illusions, suffering, and selfishness that come with it.

CHOOSE TO MASTER YOURSELF

"Knowing others is intelligent.

Knowing yourself is enlightened.

Conquering others takes force.

Conquering yourself is true strength.

Knowing what is enough is wealth.

Forging ahead shows inner resolve.

Hold your ground and you will last long.

Die without perishing and your life will endure."

- **Lao Tzu**, *Tao Te Ching*

～

We have now discussed many mindsets and methods for mastering yourself. But the most important thing to take away from it all is to remember, even as life throws countless diversions at you, what is really important. The world will tell you that you are deficient if you haven't had success in all of your endeavors. But never cave in to this narrative. Only those who have achieved greatness of the mind are worthy of our deep admiration. You will come to points where it seems like no further progress can be made. But remember that the only truly insurmountable barrier to self mastery is the failure to take on the project at all.

PSYCHITECT'S TOOLKIT

You have now reached the end of this volume of The Book of Self Mastery Quotes. If this book has been valuable to you and you would like a way to contribute, **please consider writing a quick and honest review.**

If you would like to take your pursuit of self-mastery to new heights, I write about the practice of psychitecture, or self-directed psychological evolution, which I view as the key to mastering your mind. **You can download a free, 50-page guide on psychitecture,** which includes:

• An introduction to the basic concepts of psychitecture and psychological algorithms

• A breakdown of 8 psychotechnologies you can start using to reprogram your mind

• 64 incredible book recommendations related to self mastery and psychitecture

• A list of 16 websites, blogs, and podcasts that can aid in self-optimization

• More quotes - for those who just can't get enough of them

Just go to designingthemind.org/mastery to get your Psychitect's Toolkit

Made in the USA
Coppell, TX
27 December 2024

43586836R00089